Dr Todd Greene has constructed innovative theories for human resilience and transformation through years of collegiate teaching, research and social advocacy. Discerning spiritual and sociological truths, Dr Greene creates new bridges between theological and social scientific perspectives. He believes the highest forms of chivalry will awaken in human spirits. In his personal life, Dr Greene enjoys hiking, motorcycling and spending time with his wife, Tania, along with friends, family members and animals that share their lives.

This book is dedicated to Brent H., Randy T., Pamela E., Sanghoon L., Meg M., Colby D., Kenna W., Stew M., Tucker H., Mike S., Mike U. and others who inspired me through their chivalries of spirit.

Dr Todd Greene

THE DISCOVERY OF SPIRITUAL CHIVALRY

ENNOBLING OF THE SPIRIT, SOUL, AND RESILIENT SELF

AUSTIN MACAULEY PUBLISHERS™

LONDON · CAMBRIDGE · NEW YORK · SHARJAH

A CIP catalogue record for this title is available from the British Library.

ISBN 9781528930284 (Paperback)
ISBN 9781528966221 (ePub e-book)

www.austinmacauley.com

First Published (2019)
Austin Macauley Publishers Ltd
25 Canada Square
Canary Wharf
London
E14 5LQ

Countless co-workers, colleagues, friends, students, family members and authors contributed important pieces to the puzzle assembled for this book. I cannot thank everyone by name. I do, however, wish to acknowledge certain persons who have been particularly instrumental in shaping my pursuits of chivalry, resilience, spirituality and/or other themes of this book. My first boss, Lee Cameron, showed a generation of employees at the Harvester Restaurant how to be chivalrously resilient. Cliff Miller and Dr Jerry Cloyd mentored me with the chivalrous spirit of the WWII generation. Father Mark Beran and Sister Madeleine Miller guided my awakening to spiritually chivalrous traditions of the Catholic faith. My father, G. Gordon Greene, and his friends, modelled chivalric ideals of forgotten Korean War veterans. My perspectives on God, spirituality, trauma recovery and noble spiritedness were highly informed by spiritual counsellor, Michael D. Sullivan. I owe much spiritual growth to Mike. Many of my former college students offered important feedback on my "out of the box" ideas. Savannah, Allie, and Nathaniel Lindeen, my nieces and nephew, helped me to see life's mysteries through the magic and joy of younger eyes. My father, mother, Marynelle Greene, and stepfather, Ned Sharp, have encouraged my writing for many years. I owe much thanks to the editors, designers and staff at Austin Macauley publishing. Most of all, I need to thank my wife, Tania Greene, who has lovingly supported my many ventures and adventures. Tania also contributed numerous editorial thoughts and insights to the evolution of this work.

Table of Contents

(1)

Introduction: Chivalry as a Quality of Spirit

I believe the human spirit to be inherently chivalrous. Spiritual virtues, however, need to be awakened to be consequential. And once awakened, spirits need to journey with God to become completely noble. On these journeys, chivalry ultimately increases in one's spirit, soul, personality parts, perspectives, etc. A large-scale awakening of spiritual chivalry would enable the global society to better solve its formidable problems. Every challenge, however, needs a starting point. Lifelong journeys to spiritual chivalry may begin with choices of the human heart.

In terms of definitions, I view chivalry as akin to being noble and capable in attitudes, strengths, choices, intentions, etc. Spiritual chivalry awakens when the human heart chooses to give its full being to higher causes, for the right reasons. It can align and guide one's inner and outer self. Spiritual chivalry also ennobles countless other gifts and virtues. It can encourage kindness and toughness, rational thought and intuition, action and inaction.

True chivalry of spirit is certainly not limited to a gender, or to a high social status. Early definitions of chivalry, however, were. The word chivalry actually stems from a French term in the Middle Ages for horse soldier, *"chevalier"*. Cultural meanings have changed throughout the centuries. During the Crusades, chivalric ideals began to solidify through the codification of proper knightly behaviour. Christian orders began establishing their own ideals for chivalry. Their Muslim rivals did so as well. Around 1350, French Knight Goeffroi de Charny's book on chivalry emerged as one of several attempts to standardise it. Such works asserted that chivalrous knights possess martial prowess, generosity, loyalty, courage, self-sacrifice, forbearance, humility and other Christian virtues. Knights also needed to pursue excellence. Without excellence, prowess and courage would not travel very far.

Christian and Muslim crusaders were not the only shapers of chivalric ideals. Codes of chivalry also governed popular jousting tournaments in centuries that followed. Being a chivalrous tournament knight was not unlike an American football player abiding by the rules of the game. Meanwhile, the Medieval Romantic movement envisioned chivalry in extending courtesy and protection to women. Often Romantic literature revered knights as chivalrous protectors of all innocent and vulnerable persons. Like lawmen of the American Western genre, Romantic knights were depicted as the main line of defence against forces of human corruption. In legend they slew dragons. Ideal knights were devout Christians as well. In broad religious terms, chivalry was defined by sacrificial service to God.

Assuredly, many knights fell short of the ideals of the times and orders. After seizing Jerusalem in 1099, Christian crusaders ruthlessly slaughtered thousands of Muslim women and children. Books on knightly chivalry were not yet written, but much of spiritual chivalry is intuitive. Intentions matter. One can act with a warrior's valour, loyalty and self-sacrifice for idolatrous or spiritually chivalrous reasons. The chivalrous journey of Saint Ignatius of Loyola (1491-1556) is illustrative. Born as Inigo Lopez, young St Ignatius sought exaltation as a chivalrous knight. Tales of the knights of the roundtable had helped shape his fantasies. Inigo reportedly seized many opportunities to parade around in his armour. His sword and dagger were displayed for all to see. He had the prowess to back up his vanity. Inigo had won many duels. Throughout his twenties, he solidified his reputation as a strong battlefield leader.

In 1521, however, a cannonball severely injured Inigo's legs during the Battle of Pamplona. During months of recovery, Inigo read the only works available to him—the Bible and other religious books. He began to transform. Inigo started viewing Christ as the icon of a holier, more spiritual kind of chivalry.

His ego's fantasies gave way to a series of spiritual awakenings. In his heart, Inigo began to choose spiritually chivalrous paths modelled by Christ. Rising with a permanent limp, yet resolved to serve God, Ignatius of Loyola would find The Society of Jesus ("Jesuits"). St Ignatius's spiritual exercises and methods for spiritual discernment are still widely used 500 years later.

The story of St Ignatius of Loyola is one of many that illuminate the need to attend to a core conflict of the human heart; that is, between paths of self-centredness and/or idolatry (money, power, status, self-image, etc.), and those of a spiritual chivalry. Initially, Inigo behaved chivalrously in order to manipulate others' admiration. He met behavioural criteria for knightly chivalry of his times. Yet Inigo would not comprehend chivalrous in a truer, spiritual sense until he lay in a hospital bed and opened his heart to Christ. Then his intentions transformed. Similar conflicts transpire today in the hearts of persons all across the globe. Compared to today's standards, St Ignatius faced few distractions during his time of triumphant awakening. Today, smartphones, laptops, streaming, social media, cable television and video games add to countless worldly distractions. Yet conflicts between idolatry and spiritual chivalry continue to play out in the hearts of those attuned enough to notice.

I have heard many people voice beliefs that chivalry, in the twenty-first century US, is dead. Being old enough to have known the WWII generation, I agree that chivalrous behaviour and norms have substantially declined. At the same time, narcissism, social divisiveness and other pathologies have been increasing. Nonetheless, if chivalry is a quality of spirit, as St Ignatius of Loyola discovered, it cannot truly die. The voice of spiritual chivalry can be ignored. Spiritual chivalry can also be misguided and/or corrupted, serving the wrong causes and masters, but it is unlikely to ever truly disappear. Chivalry seems encoded in the DNA of the human spirit and/or soul.

Mystical religious traditions emphasise inner pathways of spirituality that marked St Ignatius's transformation. For example, Laleh Bakhtiar describes the mystical Islamic perspective on spiritual chivalry. In the Sufi model, persons first recover and manifest the light of their original nature (spirit/soul). The spirit then gains mastery over the negative aspects of one's personality. Through spiritual growth, all positive traits become manifest. Negative ones eventually diminish. The transforming person perseveres in these efforts until the force of his/her lower passions is conquered. Firmness becomes the person's second nature. Once this occurs, all kinds of virtues are able to become firmly rooted in him/her. He/she has become spiritually chivalrous.

Mystical paths to spiritual chivalry are compatible with many modern practises of counselling, recovery and organised religion. Recovering addicts experience spiritual awakenings through 12-step programmes. A sizable number of Americans describe spiritual awakenings as "born again" religious experiences. Efforts to master negative aspects of one's personality are aligned with addiction and trauma-recovery therapies, as well as faith-based approaches to overcoming sin. Firmness as a second nature is often referred to as character development or personality integration. Virtues that link to firmness could include "fruits of spirit" mentioned in Galatians (5:22-23): that is, love, joy, peace, patience, kindness, goodness, faithfulness, gentleness and self-control.

Highly mystical viewpoints, however, can run the risk of de-emphasising the importance of action in the external world. Long periods of prayer, meditation and painful self-work are indeed necessary for awakening, development and fulfilment of spiritual chivalry. But in most cases, spiritual resources are ultimately meant to serve humankind through purposeful action. Jesus Christ offered an iconic model of inner/outer spiritual chivalry. Christ's inner relationship with God prepared him for noble actions in the world. His deeds focused on bringing hope to the poor, healing the wounded and freeing the oppressed (Isaiah 61:1). Christ's chivalrous inner journey allowed him to fulfil his chivalrous worldly actions, and vice versa.

The disparate challenges of internal and external journeys can sometimes create conflicting mindsets. For example, strong personal agency may be needed to confront worldly conflicts with valour, hardiness, compassion, largesse, etc. In contrast, a surrendering of personal control is often needed for one to awaken, heal and transform through God. Religious groups have structured their rigor to blend these seemingly contradictory mindsets. Historically, the Knights Templar, an elite crusading force that served only the Pope, attempted to groom "warrior monks". The Templars combined martial prowess with inner contemplation and surrender. Monastic orders today still dedicate themselves to chivalrously serving people in need. They also structure much time for prayer and inner development. Modern Ignatian thought calls upon Jesuits to be "contemplatives in action".

Spiritual chivalry is borne of facing internal and external challenges with the magnanimous or generous intentions. Among other things, the human heart must choose noble intentions over idolatrous and/or self-interested ones—at least more often than not. The inherent chivalry of one's spirit may first need to be awakened in order for people to realise they even have these choices. Moreover, such choices can be more difficult when surrounding groups and cultures have lost sight of chivalry and have normalised idolatry. The highest intentions, I believe, are to love and serve God. One's calling with God helps integrate the different parts of the personality that are called through spiritual chivalry.

Spiritual chivalry can manifest itself in infinite numbers of ways. Daily sacrifices for friends and loved ones can be spiritually chivalrous. Choices to risk one's life for others' welfare can exemplify spiritual chivalry as well. Chivalry of spirit can also emanate from efforts to recover from trauma and addiction, or to improve upon sins or bad habits. Efforts to combat injustice, human trafficking, poverty and environmental destruction can foster spiritual chivalry on a larger scale. Certainly, the list could go on. True spiritual chivalry emerges in both small and epic efforts. It is worth re-emphasising, though, that persons can engage in chivalrous behaviours without being truly chivalrous in spirit. For example, I've known narcissists who act chivalrously when such behaviours elicit admiring attention. They project more impressive images of chivalry than more modest people who truly manifest it. Narcissists' chivalrous behaviours are most likely driven by idolatry of themselves rather than true spiritual chivalry.

Like many Christians, I believe that the best spiritual guide is the Holy Spirit. The Holy Spirit can ennoble seekers with spiritual gifts to help them choose chivalrous service to God over the pursuit of vices and idols. God knows spiritual chivalry best. He invented it. With that said, survival skills, strengths and resiliencies also need to be acquired for the journey of the spirit. Resilience skills create foundations for later iterations of the spirit. God can work through countless human guides and life experiences to guide acquisition of such skills, resources, insights and knowledge. Not all human mentors even need to be of chivalrous spirits.

This book is certainly not written as a substitute for the guidance of Holy Spirit or important human mentors. And I wish to insert a personal note here as well. At times I have felt uneasy with the thought of writing a book on spiritual chivalry—of all things. My mind is full of memories of falling short. I know others with more impressive resumes. Yet, amid the marked chivalry decline of our times, a great need exists for maps of what the long and arduous trail to spiritual chivalry can look like. Some kind of "field guide" for navigating the many difficult processes involved is needed. Those choosing to walk a chivalrous path will need to have some idea of what to expect. They will need resilience, tools for healing and transforming, discernment for avoiding cultural snares and pitfalls, etc. Their maps for these journeys will need to blend many scientific, religious and cultural insights. I decided I know enough about the journey to write a book I believe is sorely needed.

This book pieces together insights from my many years of personal inquiry. I have sought to know God for decades. My contemplations have spanned numerous professions, mentors and denominational views. Also, as a professor of sociology, I have absorbed and contemplated a plethora of theories/findings related to human behaviours. More personally, I have recovered from diagnoses that American culture would see as impossible to recover from. Initially, resilience was the main topic of my book. I soon realised, though, that resilience needs spiritual chivalry to travel in the right direction. When human resilience and spiritual chivalry join forces, spiritual mountains can be moved. Target audiences I have for this book include people of any social background, faith or culture who wish to turn away from roads leading toward emptiness, anxiety or insanity, and walk meaningfully with their own unique nobility of spirit.

The structure of the book ahead is as follows. The next chapter discusses why a "field guide" for spiritual chivalry is needed in the US today. Chapter three summarises findings from various works on resilience. It focuses on skills learned from social situations. Spiritual awakenings tend to occur in persons' 30s, 40s or later. Resilience skills are of great benefit to people, cultures and societies even if many spirits have not yet awakened. These skills also help persons continue to thrive after they develop spiritually. Resilient persons are better able to put spiritual chivalry into worldly actions that greatly improve lives. It is in the interests of spiritual chivalry that "resilience levels" of the culture are raised. Chapter three suggests ways American culture could increase its resilience.

Chapter four discusses Joseph Campbell's analysis of "hero's journey" mythologies. Across world cultures, journey myths and perspectives help persons develop the mental frameworks needed for facing their challenges with resilience and spiritual chivalry. The culturally universal narrative of the spiritual hero maps out common challenges of anyone's calling such as: "dark nights of the soul" and "mastery of two worlds". It also provides important insights into spiritual gifts that noble journeyers will receive. In real life, spiritual journeys will awaken every dimension of one's beings, the spirit and soul included. In light of that, chapter five describes important similarities and differences between spirit, soul and ego dimensions. When transformed, each dimension contributes different gifts and substances to resilience and spiritual chivalry. Chapter five blends holistic blueprints of the human personality together to suggest how such comprehensive transformations can occur.

The sixth chapter describes how social situations, particularly societal leanings toward individualism and collectivism, impact the states of balance between spirits and souls. Highly individualistic cultures can neglect citizens' souls, hindering developments of soul chivalry. In contrast, overly collectivistic societies can overlook needs of the individual's spirit, impeding spiritual chivalry. Spiritual Journeyers, however, find ways to develop chivalrous spirits and souls regardless of the leanings of their surrounding cultures. Chapter six also discusses how changing social structures can impact how cultures relate to citizens' spirits and souls.

Spiritual journeyers learn to replace "either/or" thinking with "and/both" thinking. Chapter seven discusses how journeyers can use and/both thinking to blend important truths from scientific and cultural paradigms, while respecting limitations of each. While facilitating mental integration, and/both thinking also allows for a plethora of mental and technological resources to join forces and assist journeyers' paths toward spiritual chivalry and fulfilment of one's calling. Chapter eight puts noble journeys into a Christian perspective. Although chivalry is an inherent quality of human spirit, only God can truly ennoble it. This chapter discusses how advanced journeyers may "individuate" from God, to some degree, and become ennobled carriers of His glory. Spiritual chivalry that is ennobled by God becomes a more powerful, inspiring, and eternally enduring quality for carrying out His work.

Chapter nine explores newer perspectives on self-control. Among other things, true freedoms are not possible without reasonable degrees of self-control. This chapter describes two separate yet overlapping systems of self-control. One system is socially interactive; the other seems to operate more independently. Individuals and cultures tend to favour one system, especially in times of crisis. Imbalances in self-control systems can lend themselves to spirit and soul imbalances. Spiritual journeyers, however, draw from both self-control systems. This allows them to become independent and inter-dependent at the same time. The chivalry of their spirits better intersects with that of their souls.

Many cultural snares and pitfalls exist for those daring to journey today. Each holds potential to hijack journeyers from more chivalrous walks with God. Chapters ten and eleven delve into two common non-functional personality patterns, narcissism and dogmatism. In many respects, narcissism and dogmatism have become normalised in American culture. Narcissists and dogmatists can be so skilled at protecting their false selves and rigid worldviews that their spiritual journeys suffer. Consequently, they can be very threatened by spiritually chivalrous journeyers and respond ferociously. With increased awareness of patterns common to narcissists and dogmatists, however, spiritual journeyers can avoid or challenge many snares.

Chapter twelve addresses spiritual gifts, benefits and blessings that flow from God to spiritual journeyers. Spiritual identities fortify journeyers while facilitating greater love, purpose, joy, dignity, fulfilment, peace and chivalry. The gift of "individualised divine consciousness" allows journeyers' spirits to take the helm; leading the overall personality toward chivalrous fulfilment of callings. All buried wounds and personality parts are eventually awakened on noble journeys. Chapters thirteen and fourteen present tools and methods for helping journeyers better comprehend, heal and transform their surfacing wounds, traumas and "shadows". Internal Family Systems theory is offered as one important resource for wound and shadow work. Newer methods for renegotiating traumas are detailed as well. These two chapters suggest how every personality part can transform in ways that facilitate spiritual chivalry for the overall, spirit-led self.

Finally, chapter fifteen weaves together key points of this book. It emphasises general perspectives that emerge through noble journeys. Among other things, journeyers' perspectives allow nobility borne of Heaven to be "downloaded". As journeyers choose chivalry over self-centredness and idolatry, at least more often than not, their hearts find what they truly seek. Spiritual chivalry can better align with soul chivalry in human personalities, groups and cultures. Many persons worldwide could experience the grace of being independent and interconnected at the same time. Love, joy, meaning, strength, purpose, dignity and resolve would increase immeasurably. The global society would stand a better chance of developing noble and effective solutions to its many problems.

Often solutions begin when persons start asking the right "how" questions. "Why" questions have important places in the diagnoses of problems. Many theories can be posed for why chivalrous behaviours have declined in the US. Yet "why" questions can become mental merry-go-rounds if they do not direct minds toward solution-oriented inquiries. Chivalry stands a better chance of awakening if persons ask, 'How can people become spiritually chivalrous in a culture that normalises narcissism, mediocrity and mean-spiritedness?' Or, 'How do people maintain enough "ego" to navigate and manage very complicated lives, yet still develop chivalry in their spirits and souls?'

(2)
A Spiritual "Field Guide" Is Needed

I often include resilience units in my college Sociology courses. Ten years ago, I determined that I would be neglecting students' needs if I did not do so. Behind their self-images, many college students are visibly deficient in resilience skills. Every semester, a sizable number show significant distress over problems that I would consider ordinary. Being a sociologist, I can easily foresee more serious stressors that they may encounter after graduation. They may experience economic hardships, divorce, workplace bullying, incivility, unmanageable health care expenses, victimisation, losses of loved ones, etc. Many seem ill-prepared to step up to the challenges of adult life. By teaching resilience, I believe I can help prepare them mentally for life.

Researchers generally conceptualise resilience as a blend of dynamic qualities, rather than as static sets of personality traits. When persons and groups are resilient, they utilise many internal and external resources to bounce back from adversity, navigate stresses and dangers and create new opportunities. Recent studies suggest that the need for resilience education in the US is increasing. Jean Twenge's new research on "iGens" is one of many that support this notion. Born from 1995-2012, "iGens" (or Gen Z) have been taking the place of Millennials in college classrooms. Twenge's findings suggest that their anxiety and depression rates are skyrocketing. At the same time, many iGens are extremely preoccupied with feeling safe. To avoid feeling unsafe, many delay adult activities. The development of their resilience skills may be delayed as well.

It is worth noting that not everyone fits positive or negative profiles of their generation. Not all "Baby Boomers" smoked marijuana. Many "Gen Xers" were not cynical slackers. Not every "Millennial" projects excessive self-esteem and entitlement. Similarly, not all "iGens" fall in line with their generation's trends. With that said, iGens are much more concerned with feeling safe than any generation researched before them. Their concerns suit their times. The US has been at war for much, if not all, of their lives. Acts of terrorism and school shootings are regular events on 24-hour media. Parents of many iGens strapped them in car seats, suited them with helmets and pads before their outings and drove them several blocks to school rather than having them walk.

Throughout their childhoods, iGens consistently received messages that the outside world is extremely dangerous; they must stay safe at all costs. Of course, some fears can be valid. Due to their particular socialisation, iGens are postponing activities that previous generations viewed as rites of passages into adulthood. They are less likely to work jobs in middle and high school, to go out with friends or date or to get their driver's licences on their 16th birthdays. In one way or another, these activities make many iGens feel unsafe. With that said, some of the iGens' safety practises link to positive outcomes. This generation is experimenting with sex and alcohol later than their predecessors were.

Rates of anxiety, depression and suicidal ideation have climbed rapidly for iGens. Twenge observed upward turns in this data around 2012, the year when one-half of Americans owned smartphones. Research suggests that after two hours of cumulative screen use a day (smartphones, TV, computers), anxiety and depression increase. The typical iGen far exceeds the two-hour limit. Interestingly enough, Twenge found that iGens are also very concerned with gaining recognition for their "individuality". The iGens are usually not as preoccupied with the self-images they project as some Millennials were. They instead turn to social media in large numbers to secure validation. Smartphones allow many to meet both sets of their perceived needs. While they feel safe at home, they can seek online recognition for their individuality. They do not need to take many risks.

Resilience, courage and spiritual chivalry, however, can exist among casualties of these generational trends. Working jobs, dating, hanging out with friends and taking other reasonable physical, emotional and psychological risks can all be conducive to learning resilience, coping skills, life skills, etc. It is worth noting that it could be fairly easy for iGens to find ways of staying reasonably safe *and* embrace intelligent risks. Fortunately, many students defy their generations' trends. A percentage of iGeners have impressed me with a courage that seems from a different era. With that said, it is not surprising that anxiety rates have greatly increased among them. Many iGens are not developing resilience in the "real world". Anxiety can be lessened through development of competencies and coping strategies. Angst that lingers can be drastically reduced through faith. Unfortunately, rates of religiosity have significantly dropped for iGens as well (to be discussed in chapter 8).

Resilience thrives in the places where life demands it. In the face of poverty, violence, disease, natural disasters, civil war and daily uncertainty, many children of the world are galvanising resilience at very young ages. In US culture, the word "resilience" is being used with greater frequency. Newscasts, talk shows, Presidential speeches, and post-game commentaries regularly pay tribute to the resilience of people who have overcome adversity. Numerous correlates of resilience have recently been identified by neuroscientists, psychologists and sociologists. Resilience has also become a popular topic of disaster and trauma-recovery research, as well as self-help literature. Many authors and scholars see resilience as one of the best resources for tackling the complex problems of our times; that is, if it can be tapped into.

Resilience has been linked to the prefrontal cortex of the brain, along with many personality qualities. More personality qualities will be detailed in the next chapter. It is worth mentioning now that resilience can be paradoxical. Resilience is solidifying, yet has a flow to it. It often generates in persons possessing "opposite" personality traits. Research suggests that highly resilient people may simultaneously be self-concerned and selfless, reverent and iconoclastic, indomitable and vulnerable, masculine and feminine, etc. These paradoxical qualities suit the resilient for surviving and thriving in harsh and uncertain times.

The more I contemplated, taught, and researched resilience, the more I became aware of the need for its spiritual dimension to be discussed. For example, my students often want quick answers to "nature vs. nurture" questions. The simple but incomplete answer is that highly resilient people carry blends of inborn and acquired resilience characteristics. Social scientific answers, however, generally overlook ways that awakened spirits and souls can contribute to human outcomes. Any true quality of the human spirit is inherently resilient, because spirits are inherently resilient. When people experience spirit and soul awakenings, inherently resilient core qualities blend with their learned and inborn "ego" traits. When this occurs, the equation becomes "nature vs. nurture vs. spirit/soul" and much more complex.

Nelson Mandela's life story exemplified for me how resilience can coalesce to serve spiritual chivalry. Mandela was undoubtedly resilient in a multi-dimensional way. His personality blended qualities of strength and mercy that some people saw as paradoxical. As a younger man, and in his years of confinement, Mandela developed a lot of hard-earned resilience in his personality. His bloodline may have also provided him with inborn resilience qualities. After years of confinement, Mandela likely awakened qualities and dignities of his spirit/soul—so resilient that that no one could steal or destroy them.

The Nelson Mandela of later years seemed to have blended the hard-won resilience of his personality, his genes, and the inherent resilience of his awakened spirit/soul. Perhaps Nelson Mandela's acquired (nature) and learned (nurture) resilience created the solid character structure needed to endure years of imprisonment. Once Mandela's spirit awakened and developed, it brought inherently resilient qualities to his foundations of inborn and acquired characteristics. One resilient quality of his spirit was chivalry. Perhaps the greatest act of Mandela's spiritual chivalry was to forgive his captors then work with them for the greater good of unifying South Africa.

At a resilience conference in 2012, I asked a very qualified speaker if she could describe the ways in which resilience can be negative. She replied that she had never even considered the question; however, I had been struggling with it. My mind had been drawing parallels between the newfound popularity of the word "resilience" and the "self-esteem movement" of the 1980s and 1990s. Low self-esteem was then touted as the root of social ills. High self-esteem was seen as the catch-all solution. With the exception of Psychologist Roy Baumeister, few asked if high self-esteem could ever be negative. Many Millennials were raised on unconditional "high self-esteem". Children were showered with praise and participation trophies long before they had humility and self-control in place to handle it. Not surprisingly, narcissism and entitlement peaked for this generation. As the word resilience started to trend, I was concerned that parallel consequences could result.

My research on homeless and runaway youth illuminated one potentially negative manifestation of resilience. The best street survivors will likely be living on the streets year after year. One could argue that these youth were 'too resilient for their own good'. My research suggested a downside to some kinds of street resilience. In contrast, the runaways who sought help found residences, earned GEDs, gained conventional employment, etc. A more prevalent example of negative resilience, though, is now lodged in the forefront of mind. In the last chapter, I mentioned a core conflict in the human heart between paths of idolatry and spiritual chivalry. Persons pursuing idols can be very resilient in their efforts. A greedy person could develop much resilience in pursuit of money or status symbols while denying the needs of his/her and others' hearts. People can be so resilient on paths of idolatry, vice, and addiction that they remain closed-off to spiritual awakenings.

Spiritual chivalry became one answer to the question I raised. If persons are spiritually chivalrous, their inborn along with their acquired resiliencies will likely serve this. Resilience can then facilitate positive spiritual outcomes. On the other hand, if persons are not awake spiritually, their resilience skills are more susceptible to serving their "lower selves" as well as their idols. The same holds true for self-esteem. True self-esteem can facilitate spiritual chivalry, and vice versa. Less chivalrous self-esteem, however, can easily become intertwined with idolatry. Many Americans worship their own self-images because of the social recognition they have gained for them. This is not the same thing as loving and honouring the spiritually noble person that one is becoming.

Certainly, the idea that people can evolve from self-centredness to spiritual nobility is not new to American films, though it runs the risk of being forgotten. Choosing spiritual chivalry over self-centredness was a common theme of many classic American films. For example, *Casablanca* (1942) begins with Humphrey Bogart's cynical character "Rick" asserting, 'I stick my neck out for no one.' A chance encounter with his old flame Ingrid Bergman, however, reawakens Rick's hardened heart. As the plot progresses, Rick chooses spiritual chivalry in more and more of his actions. In the end he lets the woman he loves go. Restored by love, Rick sacrifices his own desires for the greater good of the WWII effort. Rick's choices then inspire Claude Rains' character to choose spiritual chivalry over his own self-protective neutrality.

A different manifestation of spiritual chivalry was presented by *Angels with Dirty Faces* (1938). In a poor New York neighbourhood, "at-risk" youth are torn between two role models. One is a priest played by Patrick O'Brien. The other is James Cagney's gangster character, "Rocky". The Father and Rocky were childhood friends. As the story progresses, the perks of a gangster's life sway the boys toward Rocky's ways. Rocky, however, gets arrested and faces execution. At the eleventh hour, his old priest friend shows up to ask him a favour. The Father's unconventional request is for Rocky to pretend to turn "yellow" at the electric chair so the boys who worshipped him will despise his memory. Only then could the boys be open to better role models. Rocky ultimately chooses spiritual chivalry by feigning cowardice in his last moments of life.

Western film heroes have often been seen as America's "knights of the roundtable". Chivalry appeared as a central theme in hundreds of classic westerns. Gary Cooper's "Will Kane" manifested noble-spiritedness in *High Noon* (1952). After potential deputies retreated in fear, Kane took on four outlaws alone out of higher duty and principle. Will Kane's courage and convictions inspire Kane's wife, played by Grace Kelly, to return to a dangerous situation to chivalrously defend her husband? Many manifestations of chivalry emerged in *The Magnificent Seven* (1960). Charles Bronson's character showed spiritual chivalry by extending fatherly love to the boys of the village that the seven were protecting. His character sacrifices his life trying to protect them. Brad Dexter's character, the greediest of the seven, chivalrously gives his life trying to rescue his friend, Yul Brynner. Meanwhile, Brynner expresses noble-spiritedness by defending the poor village out of higher principle rather than for money. Most of the village men awakened spiritual chivalry by choosing to fight (and no longer let their families be victimised). The Horst Bucholz character, similar to young Inigo Lopez, wanted to be admired as a chivalrous gunfighter. He ultimately finds spiritual chivalry in putting his revolver away; choosing to share a poor farming life with the woman who loves him.

The aforementioned film characters were all depicted as very resilient. They became very memorable protagonists, however, when they chose noble paths of spirit. Themes of chivalry, and often-spiritual chivalry, guided countless classic American war movies, detective films and dramas. The contexts simply changed from the plains of the 1800s, to the battlefields of Europe, to the mean streets of the inner city. Motions pictures can be the USA's most prolific mythmaking enterprises. From the 1930s through at least the 1970s, numerous film characters became cultural icons by choosing spiritual chivalry over self-interestedness. It is likely that millions of moviegoers were inspired by these films to evaluate their own hearts' potentials for chivalry.

Classic films also depict how the spiritually chivalrous choices of one protagonist can ignite spiritual chivalry in others. In previous examples, Humphrey Bogart's choices in *Casablanca* were first influenced by the noble-spiritedness of Paul Henreid's character. Bogart, in turn, inspired chivalrous choices in Claude Rains. Gary Cooper's courage and chivalry inspired noble actions in Grace Kelly. Patrick O'Brien's noble-spirited presence ignited chivalry in James Cagney. In the original *Magnificent Seven*, noble-spirited choices and actions inspired chivalry in one character after another. Audiences would have received the message that noble choices on the part of one protagonist can energise and inspire chivalry in others.

Unfortunately, I have seen newer remakes of classic American films. The original themes of overcoming difficulties to choose spiritual chivalry, regardless of consequences, are typically downplayed or lost in the shuffle of high body counts. The best films of any culture inspire what is true and noble inside of persons. They display character development. Although themes of chivalry have declined in American films and culture, noble paths are still available for those who dare to seek them. Chivalry is an inherent quality of human spirits. People need to find some cause to awaken. When movies are good, they can help facilitate these processes.

I plan to continue teaching college resilience units as long as needs exist. Last semester, though, I spoke on chivalry for the first time. I did not wake up with that intention but the day prompted it. A blizzard drifted snow across campus the night before. Morning classes were cancelled. While plodding through waist-high drifts to teach my afternoon course, I noticed a female student standing stationary in a snowdrift. She seemed to be stuck there. One step at a time, I made my way over to her. Being in my 50s, and having already walked far, I arrived a little short of breath. I asked if I could help her. My tie, briefcase, and grey sideburns hinted that I was a professor. She gave me a bizarre and seemingly hostile look, as though I was some kind of deviant. She didn't reply. I asked her a couple of more times. She still wouldn't speak to me or look me in the eyes. She did pull out her smartphone and started to text someone. Baffled, I turned around and plodded back toward my building.

Chivalry is something one can only offer. People don't have to accept it. It didn't bother me that I didn't have to lift this student up and out of a high drift. What did bother me, though, was that she didn't have the basic courtesy to answer me one way or another—let alone to thank me for offering to help. I have experienced many discourtesies from college students over the years, but this incident still disturbed me when my class started. Fifteen minutes into my lecture, I shifted gears. I shared this story. Letting my heart do the talking, I segued into how bizarre it is to me that so many people don't recognise or respect even small acts of chivalry. I spoke at some length about the WWII generation and how their noble-spiritedness influenced the culture. Several students offered that they too have been bothered by the "chivalry decline". They clearly wanted chivalry to prevail in their own lives. Perhaps they felt a stirring of their own chivalries of spirit through these discussions. Whatever the case, I had struck a chord.

Young Americans need more than just a fire of spiritual chivalry to be lit. It's an important first step, but their actual paths to spiritual chivalry will involve innumerable obstacles and challenges. Every aspect and dimension of their personalities will be tested. Some kind of atlas, that blends knowledge from numerous sources, is needed to help young adults map out where they are and where their journeys may be heading. That lecture convinced me that there's a significant need for a book to be written about spiritual chivalry.

(3)
Qualities of Highly Resilient Persons

Resilience skills are needed for most or every stage in human life. Most persons in the world will need a lot of resilience long before they awaken spiritually in their 20s, 30s, 40s or later. Resilience developed earlier in life, when persons' "egos" are in charge, lays much groundwork for spiritual chivalry to flourish later on. Without resilience, spiritual virtues may lack connecting points to ground themselves in human affairs. On the other hand, resilience without spiritual chivalry may actually perpetuate addictions, vices and idolatry. This chapter focuses on what resilience literature suggests can facilitate the development of human resilience.

Rarely has social research used the words "chivalry" or "noble-spiritedness". These concepts could be somewhat challenging to define and measure. Also, social scientific microscopes are not designed to assess qualities of human spirits and/or souls. The few social thinkers who comment on chivalry tend to cast it in a negative light—as archaic sets of norms that have perpetuated male oppression of women for centuries. Social scientific research has, however, generated numerous important findings on related concepts such as self-efficacy, prosocial behaviours and altruism. Resilience in particular has received much attention in recent years.

It is worth noting that social scientists evaluate their uses of theoretical perspectives as well as the quality of their data. Every social scientist knows the perspectives he/she employs will influence the kinds of findings that come to light. Each theoretical perspective can illuminate some aspects of resilience. No paradigm, however, can shed light on all of its dimensions. In general, sociological perspectives can highlight ways that resilience may vary by age, gender, socio-economic status, race/ethnicity, region, etc. Psychological theories seek to identify internal characteristics of resilient individuals such as flexibility, emotional regulation, "opposing" personality traits, etc. Combined perspectives can illuminate many important internal and external correlates of resilience.

Also, scientific paradigms are not the only "lenses" that can be used to view resilience, chivalry and life in general. World religions have recognised and inspired resilience (and spiritual chivalry) for centuries. Biblical stories of Job, Daniel, Joseph, Noah, Sarah, Moses, Abel and Paul are among many depicting resilience in noble service to God. The Catholic faith venerates more than 10,000 saints. Profound acts of spiritual chivalry are common routes to sainthood. Among other religious views, Confucianism asserts that, 'Our greatest glory is not in never falling, but in rising every time we fall.' Native American religions may emphasise the resilience of all lifeforms. These perspectives illuminate how plants grow back every spring, while animal species show great flexibility in their approaches to survival. Most religious perspectives "see" human spirits and souls and try to speak to them.

With that said, religious paradigms are not nearly as attuned to the worldly nuances of resilience as social scientific ones can be. Theologies are less likely to consider how cultural, environmental, psychological and physiological forces can foster or dissuade resilience. In addition, unhealthy religious perspectives can have negative impacts on resilience, human agency and spiritual chivalry. For example, the perspective of some Christians holds that God does not want His followers to develop much resilience or personal agency. Such views could negate resilience, as well as parishioners' abilities to put spiritual chivalry into action. An alternative theology might suggest that God encourages resilient and chivalrous followers. They would then be able to do more of His work in the world.

The last chapter mentioned cultural perspectives of classical American films. The American Dream should also be mentioned as dominant cultural perspective. This ideology has guided millions of citizens to bounce back from adversities en route to attaining ideal houses, cars, yards, families, etc. This perspective, however, often measures the outcomes of human resilience by house sizes ánd bank accounts. The actual American middle class has been steadily declining in recent decades. Yet a stroll around a typical American neighbourhood still evidences ordinary resilience. Citizens express this by maintaining their automobiles, repairing their homes, tending to their lawns and gardens, etc. The resilience promoted by the American Dream, however, may or may not lead citizens to spiritual chivalry.

Regardless of one's mental paradigm, the resilient person's heart will need to regularly choose spiritually chivalrous paths. A person can pursue the American Dream for purposes of idolatry, such as promoting an image or collecting status objects. He/She could also purchase houses for spiritually chivalrous reasons, such as to create places of love, honour, beauty, compassion, etc. Advances in science and technology can precipitate similar choices in the human heart. Social media can be a place of narcissism or of giving others noble support and encouragement. Some resilient churchgoers may become too concerned with gaining admiration for their Christian self-images, while those who walk with spiritual chivalry bring news levels of service and understanding with them.

Within the social sciences, the "positive psychology" movement ignited interests in resilience research. By the 1980s and 90s, some psychologists had tried looking solely at human pathology. They believed that patterns of positive mental health and well-being also needed to be unveiled. Al Siebert was one pioneer. Earlier in his life, Siebert observed that war veterans shared a hard-to-pinpoint quality that seemed to allow them to persevere through life's challenges. Siebert labelled it resilience. He could also have called it spiritual chivalry. An inspired Siebert devoted his career to exploring these qualities. He later founded The Resilience Centre and developed online resilience self-tests.

A certain "profile" of qualities of highly resilient persons emerges from a vast pool of literature that has followed Siebert. It is not this book's objective to offer a complete list of qualities potentially linked to resilience. Some correlates believed to be indispensable by some authors are downplayed by others. Other aspects of resilience still remain mysterious.

Instead, this chapter will draw from the literature to profile resilience as it could be generated in cognitive, emotional, social, and agential domains. Ways of increasing the "resilience level" of society will then be posed. Relationships between resilience characteristics and spiritual chivalry will then be suggested.

Numerous ways exist for human minds to generate resilience. For starters, resilient persons tend to maintain a realistic optimism in their thinking. Although acknowledging life's negatives, they hold onto basic beliefs that better paths will eventually appear. Many resilient people possess mature self-awareness and mindfulness. Their minds also know how to focus on solutions. The resilient channel their energies toward the achievement of realistic goals. Resilient minds break down larger problems into smaller steps. Once they take steps, they routinely reflect upon outcomes. For example, they may ask, 'Is this approach working?' If not, they consider alternatives. Resilient people are also very versatile thinkers. Their minds are not trapped in rigid boxes. Siebert emphasised that resilient people use many different thinking modes to solve their problems. They are able to alternate between creative, analytical and practical forms of cognition.

Flexibility is considered a key quality of nearly every resilience study. American culture even warns, 'If you don't bend, you break.' A strong case for cognitive flexibility is made by Laurence Gonzales in his book on extreme survivors. Gonzales argues that a key factor in determining whether or not people survive, say, being lost in the wilderness, lies in survivors' flexibility with their "mental maps". One common error made by people who are lost is to try to force unfamiliar surroundings to "fit" their pre-existing mental maps of where they are. They do not double back. They instead wander forward trying to find something in the landscape that "fits" their mental pictures of what the terrain should look like. As their strategies fail, the lost add frustration, exhaustion and distress to their problems. In contrast, survivors sooner or later accept that they are lost. They recognise that their mental maps can no longer guide them. They possess the mental flexibility to revise their mental maps to fit the realities of their new environments and circumstances.

Gonzales described a 5-stage model for being lost in the wilderness. In the first stage, persons deny that they are becoming disoriented. They press on with growing urgency, attempting to make their pre-existing mental maps "fit" what they see. At stage two, they begin to realise they are genuinely lost. As urgency turns into panic, they begin to lose clear thinking. At stage three, emotionally exhausted people form some kind of new strategy for making the unfamiliar territory fit their pre-existing mental pictures. By the fourth phase, the lost tend to deteriorate rationally and emotionally. Their earlier strategy failed to create a "match" between their old mental maps and their new physical geographies. Finally, at stage five, they realise that they must design new "maps" that fit these new circumstances. They must rediscover where and who they really are. Surrendering to their circumstances, survivors' spiritual journeys may begin.

Gonzales noted that young children have better survival rates than those aged 7-12. By ages seven or eight, children have formed rudimentary "mental maps" of their worlds. These children more easily succumb to the pitfalls of trying to make unfamiliar terrains fit their pre-existing mental maps. On the other hand, children under seven tend not to get stuck trying to make unfamiliar surroundings fit their mental maps. Their minds have not created them. Younger children simply respond to their immediate needs. If the temperature is cold, they seek warmth in their vicinity. By doing so, odds that they will find warmth and be found improve. Adults possess many kinds of "mental maps" of their worlds. They need them to navigate social, economic and sometimes geographical terrains. Resilient adults, however, possess the cognitive flexibility needed to revise their maps when they do not fit their surroundings. This allows them to change jobs, coping strategies, goals and social identities with greater ease. In contrast, some adults can spend months or years trapped in stage three when confronted with the need for change.

Mental flexibility allows the resilient to change their approaches to meeting basic needs without experiencing extreme distress. In the late 1980s, I was given entrance into a homeless community living beneath a large US city. Over time, residents found creative means of tapping into electricity, building cardboard huts, attaining water and organising socially. They even rigged the main entrance with security systems. Every fourth stair was removed from the very dark, metal staircase that led underground. Intruders could easily break a leg. This community of homeless persons seemed to have high rates of mental illness, addictions, and PTSD. Their abilities to be mentally flexible despite their afflictions, however, fascinated me. If Plan A for acquiring food did not work (panhandling), they shifted to Plan B (dumpster diving), then Plan C (selling plasma) without losing a step.

Curiosity is another resilience skill that most all resilience authors attest to. Natural curiosity is often stifled in children with the cultural expression, 'curiosity killed the cat.' In many survival situations, however, curiosity can actually be a necessity. Curious people develop lifelong habits of tinkering with different ideas, skills, and solutions. They are comfortable with experimentation. In ambiguous and dangerous situations, these experimentation skills and confidences may be indispensable. Also, the minds of curious people create countless mental "files" for how things work. Previously acquired information about edible plants, for example, can suddenly become a key resource for wilderness survival. Survival expert Chris McNab points out that in new situations, the brain will automatically scan its archives (mental maps) to find the experience that best approximates the new situation. Curious people archive much more knowledge and coping skills to draw from.

Emotional flexibility is a pivotal resilience resource as well. Resilient persons are able to access and express a wide range of emotions. They can draw from positive and negative emotional energy as appropriate to their situations. This contrasts with persons who are overly connected to one set of emotions or the other. Some people can speak for hours about things they believe are wrong with the world, yet encounter difficulties experiencing joy and inner peace. Their counterparts can be equally inflexible, like those who only express positive emotions. They force themselves to show happiness even in situations where extreme displeasure would be justified. Both examples lack the emotional flexibility that enables resilient people to draw energy, truth, and resources from a wide range of emotions—and to shift emotional gears as survival needs dictate.

Reivich and Shatte propose that emotional regulation and impulse control are among the most important resilience resources. Chapter nine will discuss how self-control is also a necessary ingredient for chivalry. Adequately managed "negative" emotions, such as anger or fear, can be converted into fuel for surviving and/or thriving. On the other hand, a lack of control over one's anger, fear, impulses, etc. can lead to countless negative consequences. Emotional regulation and impulse control are components of a more general self-control. Recent studies have indicated that self-control is a better predictor of positive life outcomes than is self-esteem. While it is possible to be too self-controlled, resilient people are self-controlled enough to sufficiently manage their thoughts, emotions, and impulses. They utilise emotional energies without letting intense feelings sidetrack their mental focus. If their emotions do overwhelm their minds, the situation is only temporary. Resilient people make rapid self-control recoveries.

Siebert, Reivich and Shatte, and many others also highlight empathy as a resilience attribute. This correlation carries some bad news with it for US culture. Empathy decreased 40% in US college students amid the "narcissism epidemic" (to be discussed later). Many reality TV programmes depict cutthroat narcissists as "survivors". In true reality, resilient persons carry genuine feelings for others. Empathy correlates with resilience in several different respects. For example, empathy facilitates positive human bonds. Healthy relationships, in turn, assist survival in many ways. Caring for others can lend much meaning and purpose to adverse circumstances. Love can give persons compelling reasons and resolve to continue onward no matter what. The human connections facilitated by empathy can also create synergy, boosting the energies and resources of all involved.

Siebert illuminated how highly resilient people are "biphasic". In other words, resilient people manifest seemingly "opposite" traits. Resilient people are masculine and feminine, tough and soft, indomitable and vulnerable, trusting and cautious, etc. According to Siebert, their blends of opposing traits acts like the positive and negative terminals of a battery.

The opposing charges spark energy. Resilient persons use this energy to renew focus, purpose, meaning, resolve, etc. Most people have opposing traits somewhere inside themselves. The resilient are comfortable bringing them to the surface and putting them to use. Biphasic resilient people walk alone if need be, but they also collaborate well in social groups. In social contexts, the resilient seek "win/win" situations. They see how their own survival increases the chances of other's survival, and vice versa. Resilient people are also adequate communicators. They seek support when necessary and available. Having compassion, they offer support as well. Most research suggests that when people believe that they are loved, respected, and valued, even though they are experiencing hard times, they are much more likely to survive and thrive.

Human agency and/or willpower are also fertile grounds for resilience to develop. Baumeister and Tierney argue that social scientific research often overlooks the human will as a key shaper of life's outcomes. The authors found that the energy of the human will ebbs and flows throughout the day as related to diet, stress, sleeping patterns, etc. They suggest many small adjustments that can vastly improve one's cumulative willpower. The will can be energised by adding more glucose to the body, exercising, shortening one's "to do" lists, sitting up straight, being clear about one's objectives, etc. Resilient people maintain strong enough will to survive, thrive, and find solutions. They take actions and follow through; persevering despite dangers, obstacles, and their own fears. They experiment, take risks, and expand their mental maps. Baumeister and Tierney suggest that resilient persons also use their will intelligently. Aware of the limitations of willpower, they rest when fatigued. The authors, however, are careful to not over-inflate the power of the human will. Even strong will is limited in the face of large-scale social and economic circumstances.

The human will is shaped by having a sense of meaning and purpose. Resilient people try to find meaning, purpose, and opportunity amid dangerous and adverse situations. Viktor Frankl's *Man's Search for Meaning* is one great testament to this. Frankl was a Jewish psychiatrist forced into the Auschwitz concentration camp by the Nazis. His loved ones were murdered. Frankl's daily life was spent surrounded by people who were deteriorating before his eyes. Frankl, however, decided that he would use his psychiatric background to forge his own sense of purpose despite the horror and atrocity he was living. He began to ask if anything could increase the odds of surviving Auschwitz. Frankl eventually concluded that retaining a sense of meaning is the pivotal factor.

Those who found meaning in their lives, even in a brutal death camp, were more likely to live. Some found meaning in offering kindness to the suffering. Others found meaning in revenge. They vowed each day to live long enough to avenge the murders of loved ones.

Frankl survived Auschwitz. His works illustrate how noble spirit can triumph even when human beings are stripped of rights, freedom, dignity, and hope. Choosing to use one's will to find new meaning regardless of the atrocities, or to spite them, is itself a triumph. In light of Frankl's findings, I sometimes bristle when I hear students say that college is only about "getting the piece of paper". They delete so much potential meaning, triumph, and chivalry from their own academic experiences.

President John F. Kennedy spoke of crises as equalling danger plus opportunity. Resilience is generated by discovering opportunities. If one only looks at the dangers associated with the crisis, his/her mind may hop into a cycle of fear; anxiety, and catastrophising may take over. On the other hand, when one acknowledges the dangers, yet shifts attention to discovering hidden opportunities amid the crisis, he/she moves to places of resilience. People put themselves in position to find constructive solutions including spiritually chivalrous ones.

Many social problems in the USA have led to perpetual crisis states. Most Americans know the dangers. The potential opportunities afforded by these situations, however, are given less attention. For example, the American Dream no longer has a 1950s economy to support it. Amid today's global economy, other nations manufacture the clothing, televisions, automobiles, and technologies that Americans purchase. Some dangers associated with these ongoing crises include increases in crime, incarceration, divorce, terrorism, mental illness, substance abuse, family violence, etc.

Initially it may seem ludicrous or callous to consider that hidden "opportunities" may exist amid the many real and perceived dangers of societal problems. But that is exactly what I ask my students to do. My intention is for students to shift from feeling overwhelmed and paralysed to experiencing resilience. First, I give students the "danger plus opportunity" equation for American Dream crises. I then ask them to write down potential opportunities they could find amid their American Dream dangers. Common answers include opportunities for more "compassion", "service to community", "family time", "knowledge", "creativity", "time to develop skills", "freedom", etc. Next, I ask students to think about the times they have felt free the most in their lives. I instruct them to approximate the amount of money these activities cost. Some typical answers are: "fishing", "playing the piano", "laughing with family", "hunting", "reading" and "motorcycling".

Students' experiences of freedom are usually inexpensive. This activity emphasises that students will not need to lose important freedoms amid the American Dream crisis, even if they are less affluent than their parents or grandparents. It also shows students that opportunities can still exist, particularly in the ways mattering the most to them. Many students experience shifts in perspective. Some sit up straight. Their minds perceive new opportunities amid the dangers they are well aware of. They appear to be of more resilient spirit. Despite American Dream crises, students' futures can be very promising.

While there is no perfect resilience, highly resilient persons manifest a good number of the characteristics described in this chapter. Resilience is associated with curiosity, being solution-focused, cognitive flexibility, using different modes of thinking, breaking problems down into steps, reflecting upon actions, possessing adequate emotional regulation and flexibility, being empathic, thinking "win/win", seeking and offering support, being comfortable with biphasic (opposite) traits, finding meaning and opportunity amid struggles, respecting one's limitations, and maintaining the will to survive and thrive.

Unfortunately, many of these qualities have been in decline in US society. Empathy decreased 40% in college student samples between 2000 and 2010. Self-control also seems to have declined in a culture focused on immediate stimulation and gratification. Inflexible cognition seems rampant in dogmatic political, academic, and religious circles. However, increases in resilience are urgently needed by a society with a 50% divorce expectancy rate, rapidly shrinking middle class, regular public shootings, terrorism fears, normalised incivility, high prison rates, and high rates of chemical dependencies, mental illnesses, family violence, and sexual exploitation of children. Stronger cultural emphasis on the qualities that create resilience may help to counter these negative trends.

I often ask students, 'How do we raise the resilience levels of society?' The first response I hear from them is that parents need to do a better job modelling resilience. I do not disagree. If parents display poor coping skills, such as addictive drinking, abusing, blaming, etc., their children are more likely to follow suit. However, I recommend multi-faceted approaches. In addition to parental improvements, the educational system could be a powerful source for shaping resilience. For example, resilience units could be taught in elementary and secondary schools. The "Three Rs" of education could become "Four Rs". Second graders could learn resilience skills appropriate to their levels of development, as could 5th graders, 8th graders, etc. Students not learning constructive coping at home could at least become exposed to better alternatives at school. Many children of dysfunction might then stand a better chance of growing up with foundations for resilience in place.

It would be unwise, however, to over-estimate the potential powers of resilience. For example, research suggests that genetic factors account for one third of the variation between persons who develop PTSD and those who do not. Resilience education cannot change genetic predispositions, though it can lend coping tools to persons at genetic risk. In addition, increasing resilience may not reverse the widespread effects of climate change, declining wages for the working poor, systemic discrimination, generational family violence, etc. Problems more large-scale and structural require solutions more structural. With that said, large-scale societal solutions need resilient people to implement them. However, even highly resilient persons can succumb to mental illness if they are exposed to too many stressors. A highly resilient combat veteran who returns home to find his/her previous job is not available, and his/her spouse is gone, would be expected to exhibit significant distress. This person requires empathy and social support much more than to be advised to become more resilient.

In the hands of more parents, educators, clergy, managers, counsellors, etc., increased knowledge of resilience could fuel a number of positive changes. Human resilience is needed long before the spirit and/or soul awaken. Social crises do not wait for spiritual growth. Young adults are more capable of navigating life's more challenging problems with foundations for resilience in place. Families, churches, workplaces, athletic teams, etc. can work together to help construct these foundations. Schools could teach the "Four Rs". Proactive approaches could teach younger children to better regulate their emotions and impulses, to be flexible, to create meaning amid hardships, to focus on solutions, to develop biphasic traits, etc.

The best forms of resilience travel in healthy spiritual directions. Each resilience quality described could serve self-interested or spiritually chivalrous outcomes, depending upon the choices of one's heart. When spiritual chivalry guides resilience, one's "mental maps" expand to include more insights from religious, social scientific and other perspectives. Curiosity transforms on spiritual pathways, in that one becomes more curious about the ways of God, and perhaps less curious about trivial matters. Self-awareness and reflection take on new roles through spiritual awakenings. Reflective spiritual journeyers may ask, 'When it is spiritually chivalrous to be tough?', 'When is it not so?', 'When is it spiritually chivalrous to be softer?', 'When is it not so?'

Spiritually chivalrous resilient people can also draw from higher sources of self-control. Self-control, a Biblical fruit of the spirit, helps persons overcome intense emotion and vice, master their whole selves, develop in character, etc. Meanwhile, chivalrous generosity can bolster everyone's spiritual paths, rather than the ego's momentary desire. The agape love that spiritual journeyers experience increases their empathy, compassion, and meaningful soul relations. Their ability to meaningfully persevere with chivalrous action increases exponentially. God ennobles believers to forge much stronger wills for doing what is righteous and chivalrous.

By improving the ability of social institutions to raise resilience levels, US culture could also teach citizens to pay more attention to their hearts' choices. Resilience and spiritual chivalry can manifest enormous transformations in human hearts and social environments. The idea that resilience can be transformative, however, may seem a contradiction in terms. One definition of resilience means "returning to form". Transformations imply the changing of forms. Yet people can overcome adversity and transform spiritually at the same time. Some of the same resilience qualities that allow people to rebound from adversity also guide their chivalrous spiritual transformations.

(4)
The Noble Journey of
Potentially Everyone

In his study of world mythologies, Joseph Campbell offered an over-arching perspective of life that can transcend certain biases of cultures and faiths. Campbell's *Hero with a Thousand Faces* (1948) asserted that world cultures and religions have been telling the same fundamental story for centuries. This is the story of the "Hero's Journey". Harrowing quests to fulfilling one's calling have been mythologised all across the globe, in cultures past and present. The "hero's journey" is that of Odysseus as well as Indiana Jones. It is a strong Biblical narrative and a metaphor for Buddha's life. It is on the short list of that which is universal to all cultures. Ancient Greeks, Egyptians, Celts, and Incans all embraced noble journey myths. One could speculate that the desire to fulfil one's calling is encoded in the human soul.

Individuals must choose to take their journey, though. Humans have the free will to decline it. Once begun, however, the journey will guide them toward spiritual awakening, spiritual gifts, virtues, freedoms, etc. It may not be an easy one. Growth seldom occurs without adversity. However, journey perspectives lend purpose, definition, direction, resilience and chivalry to the struggles of life. Journeys require resilience long before, during, and after spiritual adventures begin. This chapter will outline common events and stages of noble journeys as identified by Joseph Campbell. Each culture's journey stories and/or myths are unique and universal at the same time. Universal is the shared premise that humans are on earth to face challenges, to grow, discover their spiritual gifts, and finally to serve other people. Unique are the particularities of each story.

The hero's journey is familiar to anyone who watches films or television, or plays video games. Journey narratives have influences decades of children's movies. Almost all classic Disney films depict journeys. So do *The Lion King* and *Frozen*. Westerns are journey films, from *Stagecoach* to *Unforgiven* to today's remakes. Beloved sports films like *Hoosiers* and *Remember the Titans* follow noble-journey storylines. Comic book characters like *Spiderman* and *Batman* represent journeyers as well. War films past and present depict noble journeys.

The basic journey storyline can be broken down into three main stages—Departure, Initiation, and the Return. Each stage precipitates a number of internal and external challenges. Although no two-journey stories are identical, most start off with ordinary life. Prior to receiving their callings, future protagonists are slightly bored and restless. They do, however, possess a degree of security in their familiar surroundings, routines, and social ties. The original Star Wars began with Luke Skywalker's humble and non-eventful life with his Aunt and Uncle. Luke's life represents the standard, pre-journey phase of innocence and sheltered security. If Luke is fortunate, though, his parent figures will have instilled resilience in him. He will soon need it. It is worth noting that the makers of Star Wars were fans of Joseph Campbell. They modelled their screenplay directly from his analyses of myths.

The departure phase begins when protagonists receive some kind of call from the universe. Often a divine hint appears earlier in the plot, suggesting that lives will soon change drastically. In "real life", callings are often initiated by a series of "stressors" such as losses of loved ones, serious illnesses, unemployment, traumatic events, etc. Such crises signal the dangers and the opportunities of departure. To resolve their crises, real and mythical persons must separate from their known and familiar lives. Their journeys will lead them to new skills, strengths, insights, resiliencies, spiritual awakenings, noble-spiritedness, and finally, solutions. In both the real and mythological worlds, however, many protagonists initially resist their calls. Many fear the unknown and resist change.

They may feel inadequate. Ordinary life is boring and constraining, but they have mental maps for it. To accept a call ensures that one will step beyond his/her comfort zone and become truly lost for a while.

Perhaps the most important decision one can make in his/her life is to accept his/her call of destiny. If modern Americans resist the call, however, their culture can guide them to a plethora of pseudo comforts and false glories that may help make non-journeying lives tolerable. Alcohol and prescription medications are readily available. So are illicit drugs. Television offers a vast array of brain-numbing channels. Dopamine, which simulates adventure, is released in the brains of millions who play video games or use smartphones addictively. It is arguably easier to decline a journey in this information age than in any other time in human history. So many potential "journey stoppers" are available. The alternative choice of stepping into the unknown is certainly not an easy one. Many valid fears will be awakened. Yet human spirits seem to truly desire fulfilment of their earthly missions. Spirits may be drawn to journeying even when human "egos" are not.

Fortunately, some persons will venture into the unknown, temporarily vulnerable, lacking mental maps for where they are heading. They find the will and courage to overrule voices in their heads that say, 'You will obliterate if you step forward.' Once journeyers take these leaps of faith, the universe responds. Higher forces send mentors their way. In Star Wars, Luke Skywalker encounters Obi Wan Kenobi. Westerns bring ageing, yet experienced, lawmen into the scene. In sports films new coaches show up to take over previously sorry teams. This also holds true in real life. Many real-life journeyers later describe how the right coach, counsellor, teacher, or boss appeared at the right time in their lives. These mentoring relationships provide the bonds, skills, confidences, resilience attributes, and/or opportunities they will need for their challenges ahead.

Learning much from their mentors, protagonists prepare to cross their first major threshold. They enter into new spiritual and geographical territories, beyond the known limits of their previous worlds. Although new frontiers are ridden with snares and dangers, their mentors have taught them well. However, before journeyers are fully ready to battle outlaws, opposing armies, forces of evil, or superior athletic teams, they must conquer "demons" inside of themselves. They must spend time in solitude looking inward. The inner work of spiritual chivalry is often referred to the "dark night of the soul". If journeyers do not master their own shadows and weaknesses, their adversaries likely will. Many of the great world leaders, from Jesus Christ to Gandhi to Nelson Mandela, learned to master their inner selves in places of solitude. Periods of solitude were also structured into the rites of passage that world cultures once employed to guide young persons into adulthood.

In the second major stage of Campbell's analysis, protagonists begin their "road of trials". They may still make novice mistakes. In Westerns, neophyte gunfighters still fire some wayward shots. Luke Skywalker experienced a learning curve in mastering "the Force". Athletes in sports films have to learn to take orders and harness their raw aggressions. Mentors may still come to heroes' aid at this stage. But in myths and real life, mistakes can be great teachers. During this stage protagonists may also experience the transformative power of love. Luke Skywalker meets Princess Leia. By connecting with her divine feminine energies, Luke's motivations transform. He becomes driven to serve something greater than himself, the "Force". Over time, the power of love causes lower motivations give way to more spiritual ones.

The "road of trials" may also involve challenges with father figures. In mythological symbolism, fathers hold power over life and death. Many real and mythical protagonists are wounded by their fathers. The wounds, however, are journey necessities as well. Wounds serve to destroy the "lower self" in order for a higher, spiritual self to take its place. The need to confront a harsh truth about one's father can have such an impact. Luke's realisation that Darth Vader is his father precipitated a symbolic death of his lower self.

The road of trials grooms protagonists for their "Supreme Ordeals". These ordeals will present the most difficult tests to date. To survive their supreme ordeals, protagonists will employ every skill, tactic, experience, and power that they have acquired. At first the odds will seem against them. In Western films, the Supreme Ordeal is the showdown. In sports movies, it is the championship game with the superior team. The successful conclusion of the ordeal is the high point of the film. It is what audiences are most likely to remember. Heroes prevail. A period of exuberance follows. Yet in world mythologies, victorious heroes are also offered spiritual gifts. These gifts come in infinite numbers of forms including wisdom, power, strength, compassion, etc. Spiritual gifts are meant to reside in the holes once created by wounds and traumas. Weaknesses transform into sources of brilliance. James Earl Jones, the voice of Darth Vader, transformed his wound of a childhood stutter into a brilliantly powerful voice.

After the triumph of the Supreme Ordeal, American films may roll their credits. In world mythologies, however, the journey is far from over. Sooner or later heroes will be called to return home. The final stage in Campbell's analysis is The Return. Many journeyers first resist the idea of going home. These heroes have been on mountaintops. They have journeyed close to divinity, receiving spiritual gifts and blessings. They have also experienced the blissful triumph of victory, reaching pinnacles of some kinds of personal glory. After all of this, to return to the mundane worlds they once knew may seem unappealing at best. However, spiritual gifts and powers are meant to be used in chivalrous service to others. Spiderman is informed, 'With great power comes great responsibility.' Destiny points home. A greater glory of God will eventually find them.

According to Campbell, the homecoming is the hardest part of the journey. For starters, townspeople back home may not appreciate the returning hero's presence and accomplishments. Many people have not chosen to journey themselves. They may envy, resent, or even fear the heroes' spiritual chivalry, gifts, and powers. The spiritual energies of the hero may elicit anxiety and/or contempt in townspeople. The really fearful may attempt to ostracise or kill the returning hero. Christ, his disciples, Gandhi, and many others encountered violent reactions where hugs could have been expected. The Bible mentions that prophets will not be revered in their own hometowns. This may hold true for Campbell's heroes as well. Homecomings can offer many moments of loneliness, disappointment, and alienation. Nonetheless, journeys provide the spiritual protagonists with the skills, gifts, resiliencies, and resources they will need for their challenges ahead.

Some gifts of spiritual journeys are individualised. Others are more generic. Of the latter, journeyers ultimately become "masters of two worlds". Their challenges have taught them how to navigate spiritual realms. They also know how to manage conventional life. The spiritually chivalrous live "in" the world but are no longer entirely "of" the world. Journeyers are also blessed with the gift of internal freedom. Conquering one's fear of death creates internal freedom; so does healing from one's wounds. Mastering one's shadow is liberating. Choosing to serve higher causes is freeing. So is awakening one's spirit and soul. Stronger connections with God, in turn, amplify and add to all of these freedoms. Homebound journeyers are able to keep their internal freedoms even if they become imprisoned and/or surrounded by adversaries still trapped. Their spiritual chivalry allows them to use this freedom wisely and graciously.

Real world crises typically inaugurate journeys. Serious crises can knock persons out of their equilibriums, prompting them to choose their journey or to not do so. Noble journeys can be initiated by experiences of divorce, loss, physical injury, chemical dependency, war, crime victimisation, unemployment, etc. The particular type of crisis is less important than a persons' decision to journey. On the journey, spiritual gifts will eventually fill many holes created by the wounds and traumas. Every unique combination of wounds and gifts qualifies journeyers for distinctive destinies. Persons called upon to become drug/alcohol counsellors, for example, may first experience crisis related to their own addictions. Their departures, in turn, may begin with bottoming-out experiences. Their roads of trials may involve treatment and facing the challenges of the 12 Steps. Their mentors will appear as sponsors and counsellors. Along the way these persons may acquire higher gifts of empathy, insight, better coping, patience, etc. that enable them to fulfil their callings as effective counsellors.

In my opinion, the largest differences between people are based not on race, religion, culture, gender, socio-economic status, sexual orientations, etc., though these factors can certainly matter. The largest difference between people stems from whether or not they choose to journey or not. Journeyers inevitably become more whole, liberated, spiritual, virtuous, reverential, resilient, chivalrous, etc. Indeed, they still possess human flaws. But those who avoid their callings seem to fall more into darkness, fear, contempt, hedonism, etc. each year. Some spend lifetimes refusing to journey. On my own path, I have encountered countless people, from every walk of life, who are journeying to overcome depression, alcoholism, cancer, obesity, joblessness, addiction, various traumas, phobias, etc. Embracing journey perspectives, they improve resilience and grow holistically through chivalry. Their wounds may or may not completely heal, but these persons' spirits will triumph.

It is worth noting that Campbell's processes are very similar to the Sufi model of spiritual chivalry mentioned in Chapter one. Noble journeys awaken their true selves, the lights of their original nature. They gain mastery over the negative aspects of their personalities, eventually becoming "masters of two worlds". Dark nights of the soul can initiate these processes. Positive traits become manifest, including newer spiritual gifts. Firmness becomes the person's second nature. Once this occurs, all kinds of virtues are able to become firmly rooted in him/her. This sets the stage for freedom to live. Yet Campbell's model suggests that spiritual chivalry emerges from internal and external challenges, and ultimately leads toward some kind of service to others.

In Joseph Campbell's writings the journeying hero had a thousand faces. Motion picture industries have added a few thousand more. Through films, religions, music, folklore, and history, noble journey perspectives have offered hope, courage, dignity, resilience, compassion, resolve, faith, optimism, etc. to countless people throughout the ages. They have offered mental maps for countless blends of spiritual chivalry. Perhaps some of the popularity of American film—Disney movies, war films, romantic comedies, sports movies, adventure films, etc.—stems from the fact that audiences worldwide know intuitively that they too have callings to fulfil. Their own spirits may be stirred by the films. Psychologist Carl Jung once said, 'We are all living a myth.' If a person can watch a particular movie repeatedly, this film is perhaps telling him/her something about his/her own journey ahead.

The truest spiritual paths lead persons closer to God. They facilitate awakenings and transformations along the way. To move toward God, however, journeyers may need to step away from various social conventions. The Bible reveals numerous examples of Jesus Christ instructing his followers to transcend conventions of the times. Christ suggested to potential followers that they sell everything they have and give it to the poor to attain treasure in Heaven. He modelled loving one's enemies and praying for one's persecutors. Jesus Christ treated lepers and prostitutes with mercy, while chastising conventional moneymakers.

Spiritual journeys can be described as "trans-conventional". They include conventional structures, philosophies, practises, rules, wisdoms, etc. But they also transcend them. When spirits transform, they ignite similar growth processes in human hearts, souls, psyches, etc. Hearts may awaken truer desires to love unselfishly and chivalrously. This runs counter to some narcissistic strains of individualism in US culture. Spiritual journeys prompt buried wounds to surface and heal. To truly heal, however, a journeyer may need to transcend conventional therapies that promote medication and little else. Spiritual journeyers may be compelled to go beyond the numerous dogmas of conventional culture.

The non-journeying majority of a given group or society may take issue with journeyers' trans-conventional ways. Albert Einstein once stated, 'Great spirits have always encountered violent opposition from mediocre minds.' Greatness arises from spirits and souls, awakened on noble journeys. Violent opponents of spiritual journeyers are often "hyper-conventional" persons. Like the famous Pharisees of Biblical times, hyper-conventional people experience intense anxiety over thoughts of doing things "out of the box". The mental and emotional realms of the hyper-conventional are anxious and/or rigid. Their egos fail to recognise darker agendas within themselves. They may don masks of chivalry as they scapegoat persons of true spiritual chivalry. Meanwhile the spirits and souls of hyper-conventional people slumber.

For clarification's sake, journeyers are not automatically opposed to human conventionality. Persons who are may be described as "hyper non-conventional". Noble journeyers realise that healthy childhoods warrant significant degrees of conventional knowledge, interactions, schedules and structures. Also, children's cognitive development seems to require periods of "black and white" thinking. The conventional skills, strengths, wisdoms and resiliencies many children acquire can create enduring foundations for navigating their adult lives. At some point in adult development, however, spirits and souls begin to awaken. Spirits may yearn to move beyond conventional trappings into realms of higher love and chivalry. Souls long to go deeper in meaning.

(5)

Spirit, Soul, Ego and Personality Parts

This chapter pieces together something of an integrated map of the total human personality. As mentioned, noble journeys awaken every dimension of the human self. Spirits and souls awaken. Hidden wounds, impulses, vices and/or positive personality parts also unexpectedly rise to the surface. To some degree, journeyers' overall personalities may fall apart. This is a necessary step toward a more complete personality coming back together. During transition periods, it is especially important for journeyers to keep their focus on God. Insecurities, vices and bad habits may all become amplified. There can be danger to spiritual awakenings, though they accompany eternal opportunities.

Few academic personality theories account for the human spirit and/or soul. Psychology, for example, focuses mainly on observable personality dimensions like traits and dispositions. Theologies, on the other hand, do emphasise spirituality. Yet many religious traditions do not differentiate the spirit from the soul either. Once I asked a knowledgeable retired minister for his views on how spirits and souls differ. He had never contemplated the question. Certain Bible passages, however, speak of spirit and soul differences. Hebrews (4:12) describes the word of God as "piercing even to the dividing asunder of soul and spirit". This suggests that spirits and souls are separable yet "overlapping". Each seems to possess its own concerns, longings and needs. When their needs go unaddressed for too long, spirits and souls can even pull personalities in different directions. Ultimately, on noble journeys, spirits and souls transform and become synchronised forces of chivalrous intent.

John Woodward described a Biblical personality model that spoke to spirit and soul differences. He first detailed a longstanding debate in Christianity between two-part and three-part personality models. Two-part personality models suggest that humans are composed of spirits and bodies. Here the spirit and soul are seen as the same thing. In contrast, three-part models see human personalities as composed of body, a soul and a spirit. Spirits and souls compose distinct human dimensions. They serve different yet overlapping roles. In three-part theories, the body houses instincts, impulses and basic drives. The soul is composed of one's emotions, intelligence and will. It is a human trinity within a human trinity. The spirit, in turn, is concerned with human heights and depths. The human spirit connects more directly with the Holy Spirit than do the other dimensions.

According to Woodward, the three-part model of the spirit, body and soul was prevalent in early Christianity. Around 400 A.D., however, the two-part model began to assume dominance which continues in many religious circles today. Three-part models account for more human complexities. They offer better blueprints for human transformations. Woodward's three-part model proposes that spirits need to undergo holy conversion processes in order to receive certain gifts and powers. Spirits awaken to assume leadership roles in the overall self, to become "captains of the soul" (the will, emotions and mind). As souls transform, they become better regulators of the impulses and instincts of the "body". Meanwhile the body may also transform to better serve the spirit, soul and calling.

Biblical personality theories do not assign places for human egos to reside. Yet many psychological theories view "the ego" as an integral dimension of human personalities. The ego is tied to persons' identities and abilities to function. Susan Rhodes, however, offers a theory that integrates the ego with the spirit and soul. Rhodes maps the spirit, the ego and the soul in descending order. Representing human heights, the spirit is placed above the other dimensions. The ego lays in-between the spirit and soul. The soul, in turn, represents the domain of human depths. Rhodes proposes that each dimension carries its own purposes, limitations and even consciousness. In some regards, each dimension serves as a "checks and balances system" for the other two.

Rhodes describes the spirit as being non-material. It is a person's truest and most essential self. Spirits carry inherent desires to ascend. They long to transcend wounds and barriers, to attain clarity, to lead the overall self in Godly directions. Rhodes also argues the spirit is inherently independent. Spirits can prompt the rest of the human self to move in liberating directions. The soul, on the other hand, is more concerned with human depths according to Rhodes. Healthy souls ground people in relationships, commitments, causes and noble sacrifices for others. Souls provide empathy, compassion, interpersonal meaning, passions and humanity. In Rhodes' view, souls are inherently inter-dependent; that is, inherently driven toward connections with other's souls and life forms. In this model spirits and souls can indeed travel in different directions. Souls are drawn toward depths, emotional connections and bonds. Spirits seek heights and independence.

The human ego can be challenging to define. Panache Desai suggests that even discussing the ego is a bit like handling sand. Nonetheless, many functions of the ego have been proposed by psychological theorists. Egos help people to solve survival demands and needs. They prompt individuals to pay bills, go to work, slow down when speeding, check the oil and tyres, maintain vigilance around danger, strategise, etc. Egos operate self-navigational systems. They help persons to navigate challenges, conflicts, competing needs, priorities, etc. Egos can also be negotiators. As in Freud's view, egos negotiate the costs and benefits of various human impulses and decisions. Egos may also negotiate self-interests with the needs of others. Rhodes suggests that egos also mediate the different desires of spirits and souls. Egos can prompt spirits to temper their desires for independence in order for souls to build human connections, and vice versa.

In the pre-journey personality, human egos occupy the driver's seat. This stage of development is necessary. Most persons need a lot of skills, masteries, confidences and abilities to survive and thrive in a very complex world. Once journeys begin egos are confronted with new sets of challenges. Egos need to relinquish control, at least at times, in order for spirits and souls to awaken. If a person's ego is unwilling to step aside, spirit and soul development can be stunted. So, while helping people to survive, egos can hinder growth. This especially holds true when egos are too fractured or held together too tightly. For example, many egotists live out of touch with their spirits and souls. Their spirit and soul deprivations are casualties of their egos' competencies at the helm. On the other hand, persons with shattered egos may lack the basic togetherness needed for navigating earthly demands of life.

Perhaps the best ego condition for beginning a journey is one of a slightly wounded yet still functioning ego. The functioning aspects of the ego continue to help people meet timelines, pay bills, negotiate multiple demands and so forth—while undergoing intense spirit/soul awakenings. On the other hand, the ego's wounds can lead to humility and a greater willingness to relinquish control and/or seek guidance. Egos' wounds also open up pathways to the spirit and souls. These pathways, in turn, can lead to deep human connections and truly liberating spiritual experiences. Nonetheless, egos still need enough togetherness to help meet survival needs in complex societies.

Egos' identities are inherently incomplete. To solidify, egos will identify selectively with certain feelings, self-images, thoughts and intentions. Yet no ego could be integrated enough to govern all aspects of one's will, mind and emotions, let alone one's body and spirit. If an ego was powerful enough for full governance, it might never surrender the helm to the spirit. To manage the human self as well as they can, egos cast unwanted personality fragments into the "shadow". These personality parts go underground in the person's system. They may stay there for years. During spiritual journeys, however, buried fragments of the mind, will and emotions resurface. Healing and recovery processes ensue. With guidance from the Holy Spirit, the human spirit gains ability to govern parts of the personality that the ego could not.

Egos are also changed by spiritual transformation processes. Deepak Chopra suggests that egos shift to advisory roles when spirits begin to take the steering wheel. Slowly but surely, ego defers control to spirit. Yet most of the navigational skills, competencies, resiliencies and brain pathways forged (when the ego was in control) will still be well utilised. Since spirits do not typically awaken until persons are in their 20s, 30s, 40s or later, ego leadership is a necessary developmental stage. Some dimension of the human personality needs to navigate. And the need for earthly skills will continue long after the ego moves over to ride shotgun. Even spirit-led personalities need to budget their finances, check the oil in their cars, resolve various disputes, clean their residences, etc.

With that said, the human ego is sometimes demonised by popular culture, 12-Step groups and even some authors of spiritual development. Some confuse the ego, the necessary captain of the pre-journey self, with egotism. For example, I recall members of Alcoholics Anonymous telling me that E.G.O. stands for "Edging God Out". Spirituality authors have proposed that the ego and the spirit "cannot occupy the same house". These views imply that one cannot be spiritually awake and possess a "lower" navigational system at the same time. Moreover, a professor I knew used to shame his college students for being "stuck in their egos". This would-be guru touted the virtues of transcending the ego in ways that were reckless and inappropriate. To a large degree, 22-year-olds have little choice but to rely upon their egos. This professor wanted his students to transcend their egos to bolster his own self-image as a guru. He clearly had not yet transcended his own ego's desire to be powerful and admired. Years later I heard that he found God. Perhaps his errors led him to a healthier understanding of egos and spirituality. The spirit needs to awaken on God's timeline for the ego to have something to transcend toward.

An enlightened person once offered me the expression, 'You have to be somebody before you can be nobody.' People need to develop adequate egos before considering transcending them. As mentioned, a number of ego functions are needed for persons to maintain employment, pay bills, protect themselves and others, meet physical health needs, manage time and responsibilities, etc. In early stages of spiritual awakenings, egos also give people something to come down to after heightened spiritual experiences. The human need for an ego is somewhat analogous to that of a physical body. Humans need their physical bodies until God decides they no longer do. Humans need their egos to hold the reigns until their spirits have developed enough to co-govern.

To truly transcend the ego, in the right ways for right reasons, requires multi-dimensional growth. The human spirit needs a strong relationship with the Holy Spirit before leading the personality. To complicate matters, spirits, egos, souls and bodies can all have their own wounds and places of darkness. Spirits need to reconcile their dark sides in order to steer the overall self in Godly directions. These processes may begin during "dark nights of the soul" but can last for decades. In the interim, it may be better for a wounded ego to drive the personality than for a corrupted spirit to. Navigational errors in the spiritual domains can be consequential. Not everything in spiritual worlds is Godly. Egos are unlikely to make costly spiritual errors. On the other hand, egos are much more likely to succumb to sins and idolatry than are spirits at the helm.

The premiums I place on spirits guiding growth, however, may also conflict with some religious views. As mentioned, I have encountered many Christians who view God as not wanting His people to possess much autonomy or resilience. Leaders of one denomination, for example, consistently instructed their congregations to let Christ take the steering wheel. In figurative terms, this metaphor clashes with my belief that God empowers followers with a degree of personal agency. I consider the title of Robert Lee Scott's WWII novel, *God is my Co-Pilot*, to be a better metaphor. This suggests that God empowers journeyers with navigational skills while still joining them. God knows how to guide human agency without disrupting His connections with His people. Autonomous and empowered disciples can do more of God's work.

Any personality theory that includes the spirit and/or soul would pose challenges for conventional scientific methods. If spirits are immaterial, they cannot be seen or studied directly. Nonetheless, people can study themselves for evidence of their spirit and soul. When writing this chapter, I monitored myself for several weeks. Quickly I detected that an essential part of me strongly values independence. For years I have taken daily walks, runs, drives, or motorcycle rides. These moments allow my spirit's consciousness to rise up, experiencing new heights and freedoms. I noted that, when in the mind-set of my spirit, I am particularly determined to overcome unnecessary barriers in my life. My spirit's intention to transcend wounds and injustices seems inherently resilient. It has always been somewhere inside of me. I can neglect my spirit. Sometimes life dictates I delay spiritual gratification. But when I give licence back to my spirit, it resumes its inherent drive to transcend.

A different part of me seeks meaningful connections. I noted that in my soul's consciousness I am more concerned with creating quality time with my wife, cats, friends and other loved ones. My soul seems more directly interested in protecting, serving and sacrificing for others than my spirit is. Its intentions to create meaningful connections also seem inherently resilient. My soul's desires to connect with loved ones will be there tomorrow. On the other hand, the consciousness of my ego focuses on finding solutions to this worldly challenges. I observe my ego organising energy and resources to take needed actions. My ego also negotiates. It sets aside times for my walks (spirit), deeper connections with others (soul) and for managing practical details. Finally, I note a dimension of instinct and impulse that seems separate from the others. My body lets my ego know when I need to eat, sleep and take note of potential dangers.

Internal Family Systems (IFS) theory, founded by Richard Schwartz, offers an extremely insightful model for guiding human transformations. "IFS" asserts that it is normal for people to have multiple personalities; that is, for different parts or sub-personalities to be active within them. IFS theory differentiates several different parts of the personality. For example, Exiles are personality parts that have been intentionally driven underground in the system. Often Exiles carry intense pains, fears, shames, traumas, etc. When Exiles resurface, they threaten to overwhelm the mind with their emotional intensities. IFS also distinguishes two different types of "Protector Parts". "Managers" aim to prevent Exiles from resurfacing. They engage in a lot of proactive behaviour to keep Exiles at bay. Despite their efforts, though, Exiles still find ways of rising to consciousness. Exiles strongly want to be heard and embraced. If an Exile slips past the gates, a different kind of Protector Part, "Firefighters" steps in. Firefighters respond to threats and do damage control.

To illustrate, say a person carries unhealed exiled wounds from being shamed for being overweight. The thought of going to certain public places today, where he/she could again be judged or criticised, may activate his/her exiled childhood feelings. As mentioned, Exiles threaten to overwhelm the mind when they surface. This person's Manager Parts will try to prevent this from happening. One Manager Part may advise the person to avoid certain places. Others may try to implement diets. Despite the proactive efforts of many Manager Parts, though, Exiles can still get activated. This person could stay home yet see something on TV which triggers his/her Exiles. When this occurs, Firefighters may hop in to handle the damage. One Firefighter might try to divert the person's attention to other activities. Another might generate protective anger at others for being so judgmental about weight.

Internal Family Systems theory stands in contrast to dominant viewpoints that pathologise addictions, disorders and mental illnesses. To IFS theory, self-abusive behaviour, OCD, critical voices, grandiosity, alcoholism and manic episodes would all be seen as Protector Parts. For example, many alcoholics try to function by exiling pains, fears, disappointments, angers, sorrows and traumas. As these Exiles begin to rise up, alarm bells may sound throughout the personality system. An alcoholic Protector Part may step in. Intoxicants quickly quell the emotional intensity of resurfacing Exiles. Alcohol consumption also protects by allowing one to feel he/she has control over deeper distress. Meanwhile, the mind of the alcoholic may focus on acquiring another drink. This too serves protective purposes. This mind is directed away from resurfacing emotions and traumas, the intensities of which may threaten survival, sanity, dignity, etc.

Protectors and Exiles are important parts of the true self. IFS theory, however, sees the true self as more than the sum total of its Protectors and Exiles. A deeper, more essential self is believed to exist. This view is compatible with religious perspectives across countless cultures. Richard Schwartz and Robert Falconer argue that whether the true self is called the

Atman, Te, Inner Light, or Spark of the Soul, most cultures believe humans possess a deep and indestructible essence. Schwartz and Falconer propose that true selves (spirits) possess a number of inherent qualities. Initially referred to as the "8 Cs", these qualities are calmness, curiosity, clarity, compassion, confidence, creativity, courage and connectedness. I would add chivalry as a 9th inherent C word of the spirit. Recently IFS authors have added joy and harmony to their list.

It is worth noting that IFS believes that as Protector Parts learn to relax, and Exiles begin to heal, the true self (spirit) will awaken. Eventually the true self will assume the helm of the overall personality. IFS theory calls this self-leadership. Self-led persons are filled with self (or spiritual) energy. They learn to tap into their own wells of calmness, curiosity, clarity, compassion, confidence, creativity, courage, connectedness, joy, harmony and chivalry. Over time, Protectors that have engaged in maladaptive behaviour can transform in ways facilitative of chivalry. Through self-dialogue, Protector Parts choose more constructive roles while still advising responses to threats.

What many psychological theories have called the ego, Internal Family Systems theory sees as active Protector Parts. Protectors that spend significant time engaged can easily become part of the ego's identity. For example, if one's Protector Part often uses humour to diffuse tense situations, the person might be defined as funny. If a person's Protector Parts frequently steel him/her emotionally, toughness may be part of his/her social identity. Through growth processes, however, people begin to form identities more related to their true selves (spirits). In IFS terminology, persons' true selves "unblend" from their Protectors. New identities can include, but will also transcend, roles that protectors play. The IFS model does not, however, differentiate the spirit and soul. Their true self-concept seems fairly synonymous with others' conceptions of the spirit. The soul is more likely where the substances of Exiles and Protector Parts come from. Each Exile and/or Protector may represent distinct but fragmented pieces of the human soul.

One step at a time, spiritual journeys pave the way for the restructuring of human personality. Again, egos or Protector

Parts guide personalities until spirits are ready to lead. Awakened spirits are groomed for self-leadership through their connections with God. On Godly paths spirits gain graces, powers and gifts. Egos/Protectors then transform by slowly shifting to advisory roles. Souls, in turn, transform through processes that recover and reintegrate lost fragments of the mind, will and emotions. These processes, to be described in chapters 13 and 14, often occur in the contexts of human relationships. As journeys progress, the transformed spirit becomes more involved with governing the soul. The healing soul is better able to regulate the body's impulses and instincts. Journeyers become more whole. Their chivalrous character begins to look more like their Creator's.

Chivalry can exist in every human dimension. It is noble for spirits to transform and assume self-leadership. Awakened spirits connect more closely with the holy nobility of God. Receiving guidance from the Holy Spirit, human spirits also behave more chivalrously at the helm than egos/Protectors do. Spirits chivalrously steer the overall personality toward service to God and others. Spiritual mental maps integrate conflicting worldviews. This leads to less divisive and more chivalrous discernment to see the world and other people. Chivalry is also borne in the soul. Human souls inherently seek meaning in serving and sacrificing for others. Unhealthy souls may sacrifice out of co-dependency or other insecurities. Chivalrous souls sacrifice out of higher love, for higher purposes.

It is worth emphasising that transformed spirits and souls can still travel somewhat different pathways. The cross provides a powerful symbol for spirit and soul pathways. Spiritual channels to God seem more "vertical". Spirits' inherent desires to ascend, transcend barriers and live freely travel "up and down". Soul connections seem more "horizontal". Souls seem to experience God through grounded connections with other persons, animals, nature, etc. God joins together these different pathways through His gift of calling. Through callings, each human dimension or part can choose to follow the same compass. Agreement of spirits, souls and other parts to contribute to the calling, in turn, can integrate and galvanise different sources of chivalry.

Healthy spirituality enhances the soul lives and vice versa. For example, on my daily walks my spirit typically becomes energised. Later I can bring spiritual energy to my soul's relationships; that is, my marriage, friendships, teaching, etc. Healthy soul connections inspire me in different ways through the sharing of meaning, love, purpose, etc. An awakened soul life lends much meaning and direction to spiritual self-leadership. In my best moments I can feel free (spirit), meaningfully inter-connected (soul) and ennobled at the same time. To be sure, untransformed Protector Parts still reside inside of me. Sometimes I am a bad decision away from maladaptive coping. Yet my Protector Parts respond much better to my spirit's guidance than they ever did to the dictates of my ego.

(6)
Chivalry in Individualism, Collectivism, Social Change

Chivalrous metamorphoses occur amid angst, turmoil and hyper-conventional values of surrounding human cultures. Social scientists know well that human development is influenced by multitudinous internal and external forces. Marriages and families, employment situations, race/ethnicity, gender, coping resources, genetics, age, neighbourhood, religion and social media are among the factors that influence personality development. Social conditions also impact states of the spirit and soul. Cultures that glorify the false self tend to produce more narcissists while neglecting spiritual and soulful dimensions. Other cultures over-emphasise soul dimensions. While fostering strong human bonds, they may neglect needs of citizens' spirits to be free. Meanwhile, societies over-emphasising spiritual freedom may devalue important soul relationships.

Journeyers follow, and advocate for, their own cultures' values when these lead toward God. However, when cultural pathways create unnecessary dysfunction or insanity, journeyers follow the higher compasses of their callings. This chapter describes several cultural situations that impact persons' balances of spirit, soul and personality parts. One involves strong cultural leanings toward individualism or collectivism. Another relates to impacts of various social changes. I will propose ways that spiritual chivalry can integrate opposing models of individualism and collectivism, while helping to guide societal changes.

Cultures too "individualistic" or "collectivistic" set their citizens up for specific kinds of spirit/soul imbalances. For example, overly collectivistic societies can give too much weight to the social group; not enough to the individual. Extremely individualistic cultures lean in the opposite direction. United States culture is highly individualistic. The symbol of America, the bald eagle, represents individual independence and ascension. The eagle is not a "pack" animal. The US highly admires individuals who have risen to heights in wealth, athletics, the media, etc. The American spirit's drive to ascend has taken individuals to the moon and beyond. The culture's gunfighter mythology has generated hundreds of icons of self-reliant heroes who fought alone. Many US citizens commonly espouse the rights of American individuals to bear arms and not pay too many taxes. Efforts to ensure that "big government" stays out of individual affairs can be rousing political forces.

The United States reveres the need for human spirits to ascend and live freely. It also promotes the ego's pursuit of idols and gratifications. Yet amid the processes of celebrating the human spirit, and licencing the ego, the US often deprives its soul. Widespread soul neglect can be evidenced by a 40% decline in empathy, 50% divorce expectancy rate and outspoken disdain for the underprivileged. A strong barometer of soul healthiness is how a society treats its disadvantaged citizens. Among other things, the rising number of low-income citizens indicates that the 1950s American Dream has faded. Some citizens would rather channel their hostilities toward human targets than revise their outdated mental maps of the economy. Soul neglect can also appear in high rates of alienation, anxiety/depression, narcissism, addictions, suicide, etc. These trends can reflect a widespread lack of inter-connectedness.

In contrast, many traditional Asian cultures are highly attuned to soul dimensions. Strongly collectivistic cultures tend to elevate the importance of group cohesion and harmony over the interests of particular individuals. Collectivistic family systems are more extended. The importance of honouring not only one's parents, but one's ancestors, is emphasised. Whereas US culture says, 'The squeaky wheel gets the oil,' the Japanese warn, 'The nail that stands up gets hammered down.' Collectivistic citizens share many interconnected struggles, meanings, sacrifices and purposes. A downside, however, is that the needs of individual spirits to transcend can be severely neglected. Souls, in turn, are more vulnerable to "groupthink".

Individualism and collectivism are rarely "all or nothing" though. No person or culture is entirely individualistic or collectivistic. Individuals and cultures instead possess tendencies to emphasise one model over the other. Leanings toward individualism and collectivism can change within the same culture. The US Armed Forces, for example, recruited Depression-era citizens with 'Uncle Sam Wants You'. To recruit the next generations, slogans changed to the individualistic 'Be All That You Can Be', then the more individualistic 'An Army of One'.

Individualism can be conducive, antithetical, or neutral to spiritual chivalry, depending upon its emphasis and relationship to the soul. An individualism that promotes inner paths to holistic growth, self-mastery, healing, etc. would facilitate spiritual chivalry. Individualistic spirits also find chivalry in self-leadership and higher connections with God. However, when individualism fosters mass self-centredness and soul neglect, it travels less noble paths. Darker sides of humanity are empowered when self-centred individuals refuse to serve higher causes. Collectivism can foster much of its own kind of chivalry. Indeed, it can be noble to sacrifice one's interests for the greater good of the group or society. On the other hand, when collectivists sacrifice themselves for wrong groups, leaders and causes, they enable oppressive forces to assume more power. Underdeveloped spirits may not be able to rise above this.

In following the compasses of their callings, journeyers may at times need to be non-conformists. Jesus Christ defied social conventions on many occasions. So journeyers in individualistic cultures may need to go against cultural grains to develop healthier soul lives (while still keeping positive aspects of their culture's leanings). Collectivists may need to break social conventions to develop a healthier independent spirituality. They can still retain healthy soul connections. The best forms of spiritual chivalry result from hybrids of individualism and collectivism. Spiritual journeyers embrace healthy aspects of individualism and collectivism without being extreme in either direction. On their best moments, journeyers feel independent (spirit) and inter-dependent (soul) at the same time. They feel doubly noble.

I view the "culture" of Heaven as designed to jointly meet the needs of spirits and souls. The journey of neurosurgeon Dr Eben Alexander is suggestive of this. Alexander experienced a life-changing journey into the afterlife. He had contracted a rare form of bacterial meningitis. The entire cortex of his brain shut down. Alexander was not expected to recover from a vegetative state. While brain scans recorded no patterns of activity, Alexander reported that his consciousness had not only been active but had visited Heaven. Eventually Alexander returned to his body. Alexander stated that everything in Heaven was free and distinct (spirit), yet also a part of everything else (soul). Inhabitants of Heaven were independent and inter-dependent at the same time.

One way spiritual journeyers can move in Godlier directions is by thinking "and/both" instead of "either/or". Rather than assuming one can either be individualistic or collectivistic, a journeyer is more likely to ask, 'How can I blend individualism and collectivism to create healthier spirit and soul lives?' While embracing their cultures' virtues, journeyers also develop in the dimensions their cultures de-emphasise. Spiritual journeyers in individualistic America find ways to nourish their souls. Some form "soul families" with other journeyers. Others actively participate in churches, clubs and/or community projects. Meanwhile journeyers in overly collectivistic cultures find solitary times, places and activities to fuel their spirits' freedoms and transcendence.

Economic, technological and cultural changes can also influence whether spirit and soul domains are emphasised or de-emphasised. They can also impact cultural views on chivalry. For example, relationships between factory workers and owners were once guided by the "social contract". The social contract established mutually beneficial patterns of relations. Factory workers deferred authority to management when "on the clock". They dutifully performed repetitive tasks. In return they received liveable wages and lifelong employment. The forty-hour workweek allowed workers to develop personal navigational skills in leisure time.

Management, in turn, honoured their side of the contract by staying loyal to towns and employees. They received dutiful and hard workers in return.

The social contract was not only win/win, it was conducive to chivalry. Hard work was viewed as chivalrous. So was staying loyal to the town. Duty to others and society was considered chivalrous. In addition, the social contract helped create a cultural template for balancing disparate needs of spirits, souls and personality parts. The spirits of many workers could experience energising heights and freedoms on weekends. Workers' egos earned enough money to navigate life. Families with one working parent were afforded quality time, cultivating soul connections. Furthermore, relative job security allowed workers to develop soul-enhancing camaraderie with their co-workers, on and off of the clock.

The information age, global economy and outsourcing of American jobs have nullified much of the social contract. Meanwhile the norms and values of the WWII generation, which emphasised chivalry, duty and honour, no longer guide American culture. Consequently, the rules, constraints and opportunities embedded in American workplaces have drastically changed. Such changes have impacted states of balance between spirits, souls and personality parts. American souls have lost many of their traditional relational anchors. Today's notion that everyone is out for him/herself pervades many occupational cultures and policies. Lifetime loyalty to the company or the town is seen as something of the past, even foolish. A higher percentage of American families are two-income, struggling to make ends meet. Less time and energy are available for nurturing soul connections. Empathy for struggling Americans has also declined.

Some American spirits strive for heights and freedoms without healthy human bonds to ground them. Simultaneously, numerous American egos have succumbed to cultural influences of narcissism and entitlement. Rather than facilitating spiritual chivalry, individualism has fostered an 'I am entitled to do whatever I want to do' attitude. American egos also face many new navigational challenges in the global economy. The industrial-age ego that once performed repeated tasks, never complained and rarely challenged authority, would lack important survival skills in today's society. Navigating the Information Age warrants vastly different skill sets.

Tony Wagner offered seven survival skills that he sees as necessary for navigating today's information economy. His list reads much like the resilience skills previously profiled. These seven skills are: (1) Critical thinking and problem solving, (2) Collaboration across networks; (3) Agility and adaptability (flexibility); (4) Initiative and entrepreneurship; (5) Effective oral and written communication; (6) Accessing and analysing information; and (7) Curiosity and imagination. Industrial-age egos were discouraged from engaging in much thinking or initiative on the clock. Today's workers, in some respects, need to develop opposite traits. They definitely need more autonomy, flexibility and personal control. Yet today's workers will need to create new templates for becoming independent and inter-dependent at the same time.

Wagner's list also reinforces the idea that resilience education will continue to be needed. As mentioned, many iGeners have been conditioned to avoid feeling unsafe. Resilience involves taking some risks. Chivalry does as well. Many iGens relay heavily on their smartphones to feel safe and gain recognition for their individuality. Yet in many cases, smartphones seem to be in control. Five minutes before college classes start, classrooms are so quiet I could hear a pin drop. Sometimes I drop a pen to make that point. About 80% of my students are focused solely on their smartphones. Only rarely do classmates chat with one another. This is the new normal. As I stand quietly within my own thoughts, I consider that their souls need face-to-face interactions to develop. Their egos will need more skills and resiliencies to navigate a fast-changing economy. Their spirits' inherent desires for independence will require major awakenings, probably initiated by crises.

A resurgence of chivalry norms in the US could serve as a better guide than immature strands of individualism. Those not following the compass of God will more likely follow their egos toward idolatry in individualistic or collectivistic forms. Chivalry could also be a guiding force in the social organisation of the industrial age economy. Once the social contract asked for and received chivalrous sacrifices on the parts of CEO's and factory workers. With widespread spiritual awakenings, principles of chivalry could resume such roles. If this does not happen, though, spiritual journeyers can still rely on their callings' compasses. God guides journeyers toward filling spirit/soul voids created by their cultures. He also ensures journeyers travel in noble directions, even when human cultures have lost sight of them. As more resilient journeyers embrace spiritual chivalry, their ability to impact their surrounding cultures drastically improves.

(7)

Chivalry in Scientific and American Dream Perspectives

Recently religion declined somewhat in the US, according to Twenge's generational research. The US still scores high on religiosity scales when compared to most European nations, but the number of 18-22-year olds who report "no religion" is now 36%. This figure was 11% in the 1970s. The percentage of 18-22-year olds who report never praying rose from 4% to 28%. In the 1990s some Americans reported they were "spiritual but not religious". These particular trends, however, were not driving Twenge's findings. Twenge's study suggested that instead iGeners are experiencing conflicts between faith and scientific views. Instead of seeking resolution, some are simply choosing science. Interestingly enough, most iGens still believe in an afterlife. The trend is for God to be deleted from these persons' visions of Heaven.

Of course, the idea of faith and science being at odds long precedes iGens. Over the years I have received strange looks from social scientists after mentioning I was a Christian. They seemed to think I should have outgrown my religious beliefs when I learned the Easter Bunny was not real. Another absurd assumption is also involved; that is, that I am too weak to accept harsher realities of life that they know to be true. In truth I probably understand these realities better than they. On the other hand, I have received equally troubling looks from some Christians after mentioning I was a social scientist. They seemed to think I was somehow less of a Christian, and/or some kind of deviant, because I respect scientific methods and the God-given powers of the human mind.

An "and/both" thinker can embrace science and faith. For example, many look at intelligent design versus evolution debates from an either/or perspective. Either God designed life as it is, or life discovers its own ways to evolve. And/both thinking could consider that God perhaps designed life in ways that allow it to change and evolve. This view recognises inherent resilience in God's design. Spiritual chivalry, again, is one of the many beneficiaries of and/both thinking. The worldviews of the spiritually chivalrous are less divisive. Evidence supporting one view does not need to be cast aside for the sake of a different view. Journeyers are more likely to arrive at higher truths. And these truths are more likely to lead to actual improvements in the world.

This chapter discusses how spiritual chivalry can help guide the uses of cultural and scientific perspectives. Several factors differentiate spiritual journeyers' uses of conventional perspectives from non-journeyers. For one thing, when scientific, cultural, or religious perspectives contain distortions, journeys are driven to remedy them. Secular and/or religious dogmatists, on the other hand, may just dismiss discrepancies. In using and/both thinking, journeyers seek ways to resolve conflicts between opposing worldviews. Journeyers' perspectives are also influenced by the awakened eyes of their spirits and souls; and their enhanced connections with God. This allows them to notice important details that conventional viewpoints overlook. Finally, journeyers do not need to cling to particular paradigms to find their bearings. Their compasses are set toward God. They are free to draw truths from many worldviews, yet transcend biases and limitations.

Conflicts between spiritual chivalry and idolatry certainly play out in worldviews. Paradigms of science, culture and religion can all be used for spiritually chivalrous purposes or ones less so. For example, internet technology can be used for many noble or ignoble purposes. US culture chivalrously founded a democracy, elevated human rights, established laws for equal rights and liberated other countries from oppression. Yet the same culture has given birth to a narcissism epidemic. Noble churches guide parishioners to the best versions of themselves in this life and beyond. Unhealthy ones, however, make idols out of their self-images as good Christians.

To scientific paradigms, the planet is organised and guided by discernible patterns. The studies of geology, sociology, pharmacology, chemistry, biology, etc., all analyse different patterns in systematic ways. Sciences assume degrees of predictability. Each field seeks to illuminate predictable causes and effects in their patterns of study. Meteorology strives to identify patterns that predictably produce storms. In positive psychology, patterns of flexibility, empathy, emotional regulation, etc. predict resilience fairly well. Sciences also strive to measure their patterns of inquiry. The pattern of water boiling at 212 degrees Fahrenheit can be measured by a thermometer. The social scientist administers surveys, tested for reliability and validity, to measure human attributes. By illuminating countless patterns, sciences have allowed much of the earthly world to be navigable and comprehensible to human minds.

Scientific worldviews do, however, possess inherent limitations. This is particularly evident when spirituality is concerned. As mentioned, human spirits can elude scientific assessment. Dr Alexander's spiritual consciousness did not show up on a CAT scan. Yet if Alexander is correct, his spirit travelled to Heaven and was transformed by the experience. Spiritual freedom can create problems for scientific predictability. Journeyers are fairly predictable in their efforts to serve God. Yet in their abilities to think, act, feel and navigate outside of human confines, journeyers may seem very unpredictable. Spiritual journeyers may behave even less conventionally the more they transform. It is worth noting that the most predictable persons are those enslaved by their compulsions, addictions and vices. They react very predictably to external stimuli, doing the same things over and over again. Journeyers stand in stark contrast. Their internal freedoms allow them to choose responses from a wide range of potential responses. If one strategy does not work, a journeyer will likely do something different the next time.

Many social scientific views also assume that humans are, or should be, rational. Human abilities to think rationally are great gifts, but spiritual chivalry is able to transcend this. Once journeyers awaken to agape love, they may deny their own emotional needs or ignore self-preservation instincts. In the movie *Titanic* (1997), Kate Winslet jumps back onto the sinking ship to be with her soul mate, Leonardo DiCaprio. The scene is a powerful depiction of agape love, but not rationality. Jesus Christ's immeasurably chivalrous decision to die on the cross would seem less rational to persons whose only worldview is scientific. Sciences and cultures can also be biased in their views of what constitutes rationality. Individualistic cultures may see it as rational to deny one's soul. Collectivists' may believe neglecting one's spiritual independence is rational. God's higher logic, however, is holistic in what it sees as rational or right.

Science can also create its own idolatry. Humans can over-inflate their perceived ability to control their world. Tenacious and intelligent scientific minds can become trapped in their own rationality. Yet in countless ways, sciences do lead people toward God and His higher chivalry. Using science to guide reductions in poverty, disease, violence, mental illness, etc., is very compatible with the values of most religions. It is also noble. The sciences aid complex human cultures in comprehending, guiding and caring for their surrounding worlds. I need not look far to see how I have science to thank for countless important tools and technologies in my life; and for the fact that I am still alive. Using science for spiritually chivalrous purposes is a choice made by individuals, yet influenced by their surrounding cultures. Through and/both thinking, journeyers can strike balances between the relative types of control offered by science, and the faith needed to reconcile that which cannot be controlled. Science and faith can both facilitate spiritual chivalry.

It is worth noting that spirit/soul dimensions need not be completely off limits for social scientific inquiry. For decades sociology and anthropology have documented ways in which different cultures practise spirituality. Qualitative methodologies can allow social scientists to collect and interpret indirect evidence of spiritual lives. In the US, researchers could create samples of persons who report having experienced spirit/soul events. Respondents could be asked to describe their experiences. Their interviews could then be analysed for common themes. Important patterns related to how people make sense of their spirit/soul experiences could be illuminated. While not proving the existence of God, or the spirit/soul, such research could piece together models for how journeyers assimilate spirit and soul experiences. Inspiring themes of healthy spirituality could emerge.

Culture is often defined as a total way of life of a group of people. Cultures include a group's material items, such as its tools, technologies and weapons. They also encompass non-material ideas like knowledge, values, goals and beliefs. In some societies religion and culture are highly intertwined. The US, however, has forged its own cultural perspectives aided by church and state separations. Some Americans' secular perspectives have become their dominant worldviews. Others seek ways of integrating cultural viewpoints with their scientific and theological views. Whatever the case, American culture is a complex and even contradictory blend of different beliefs, practises and perspectives. For example, America values civil rights yet carries a number of racist, sexist, homophobic, and xenophobic beliefs. Individual chivalry has been a strong theme of American film and folklore. Other cultural sources rapidly create idolatry of money, social status, self-image, power, etc., and then normalise it.

The diversity of viewpoints encompassed by American culture can cause it to mean different things to different groups. The term "culture wars" refers to ideological conflicts between liberal and conservative viewpoints on what America is. Among other things, ideas of what is or is not chivalrous can be divided along political lines. Conservative views tend to focus on the chivalry of persons serving in the military and/or law enforcement, making sacrifices to defend others against threats. Liberal views focus on the chivalry of sacrificing to help create equal opportunities for women, minorities, and sexual minorities. Both sets of actions can be highly chivalrous. My wife and I recently noted two signs on the front door of a house in Lincoln, Nebraska. The first read, 'Police Lives Matter.' The second said, 'Black Lives Matter.' This resident was thinking and/both instead of either/or.

A few cultural perspectives have been more widely accepted across lines of politics, race/ethnicity, gender, social class, etc. Perhaps the best example of this is the American Dream. For decades, this standardised dream of financial success informed all citizens that their land is one of opportunity. Any individual with will and determination could succeed in America. Success, social value, and social glory are within the reach of anyone determined to acquire "ideal" houses, jobs, cars, families, and so forth. During the 1950s, the American Dream helped the US to develop a middle-class society; a model for the rest of the world. Despite significant economic changes, many Americans today still see the world through this paradigm.

The US experienced less economic competition in the 1950s. European economies were rebuilding from WWII. Nations such as China, India, and Japan had not yet fully industrialised. The USA made most of the cars, televisions, electronics, and many other material goods. One-fourth of the US economy was involved in manufacturing. Meanwhile the G.I. Bill made college education a reality for much of a generation. Standards of living increased for the average American household every year for three decades. That economy, however, began to face serious trouble in the mid-1970s. In the 1980s, American factories moved in greater number to countries such as Mexico. Today, manufacturing makes up 12% of the American economy. For these and other reasons, the American middle class has been declining. Many Americans have felt lost.

The stages of being lost, discussed in chapter three, can shed light on how many Americans can retain a worldview that has not meshed with the actual economy in decades. A number of Americans seem stuck at "stage 3". To reiterate, persons at this stage anxiously devise strategies for making their unfamiliar worlds fit their pre-existing "mental maps". American Dream adherents may try to make the global, service, and information economies fit their mental maps of the economy and society of the 1950s (rather than modifying their worldviews). This is akin to travelling the continent with 1955 road maps. Economic realities today are quite different. I try to buy American-made products. Yet the computer I am using comes from Japan. The shirt I am wearing was made in Bangladesh. My blue jeans, a Red-White-and-Blue brand, were produced in Mexico. Meanwhile I see many former students, now college graduates, working at superstores where such items are sold.

The US economy and culture need many changes and improvements. The mental maps of the 1950s, however, will never mesh with the economic terrain of the 21st century. To move beyond "stage 3" of being lost, Americans will need to seek new opportunities amid the dangers. One such opportunity could entail revising the American Dream in ways that encompass more Americans than the 1950s version ever did. Certain blind spots existed for the older American Dream perspective. Even in the 1950s, the lives of many low-income Americans were rendered invisible by a lens that overly emphasised material success. Similarly, the belief that anyone with determination can succeed in the US has had a shadow side; that is, the fairly common perception that low-income Americans are weak-willed or lazy. Much badmouthing of disadvantaged persons, who already have strikes against them, has been rationalised by this perspective. Christ, on the other hand, showed chivalry in treating disadvantaged persons with love and dignity. The old American Dream perspective also obscured evidence of class systems in the US. Today 50 million Americans fall below the poverty line.

The United States now has opportunities amid these crises to form new, realistic, and better cultural perspectives. The 1950s American Dream ideology could be replaced by a culturally specific Noble Journey viewpoint. The journeys of chivalrous Americans regardless of race, gender, sexual orientation, etc. could be celebrated. This perspective could "judge" human dignity by character qualities rather than by skin colour or material possessions, creating less unjust shaming of the disadvantaged. American culture could still honour its frontier mythology, technological ingenuity, work ethic, pioneering spirit, etc. An improved cultural perspective could respect the gifts, strengths, virtues, and resiliencies of citizens across all lines of social difference. Chivalry could become more visible in multitudinous manifestations—rather than as existing within one social group but not another.

Another opportunity could be for a cultural viewpoint to pay more attention to the needs of American souls. If a new cultural perspective were more holistic, it could restore the soul to a proper place in American consciousness. In addition, revisions to the American Dream perspective could help renew its political functions. The American Dream once served to bridge political gaps. Both political parties could more or less unite under its visions of middle-class democracy. Parties were still divided on particular issues, but the old American Dream offered a higher means of conflict resolution. It allowed partisans to say, 'We disagree on these particular issues, but we all believe in the American Dream,' or, 'We are Americans first and party affiliates second.' Today Congress is having a particularly hard time compromising and solving problems without sharing in an over-arching cultural perspective.

With that said, spiritual journeyers are unlikely to stand idle until a divided culture revises an outdated secular paradigm. On the individual level, any person could seek opportunities right now to modify his/her personal perspectives. My college students have come up with many ideas for revising the American Dream for themselves. When asked to fill the blank of "Less materialism, more _____", they list things such as compassion, service to community, family time, knowledge, skill development, freedom, etc. Any of these endeavours could be chivalrous. New perspectives can also be more holistic in their treatments of spirits, souls and egos. Even if much of the surrounding culture is divided, journeyers can advance toward holism. If enough persons adopted "and/both" perspectives, paradigms of the larger culture may begin to transform from the ground up.

With compasses set toward God, journeyers can make chivalrous use of scientific and secular worldviews while also transcending their biases and limitations. Faith, science and culture do not even need to exist in perfect harmony to inform spiritual journeys. At times, I still struggle with conflicts between my social scientific, religious and/or cultural views. I have learned to trust, however, that God will lead me toward the right insights (often blended from many perspectives) on His timelines. The best chivalry flows from God, rather than rigid human perspectives. Spiritual chivalry can guide persons' uses of all kinds of worldviews.

In its best moments, the United States has been monumentally chivalrous. I am honoured by the nobler aspects of American culture. Sometimes the US has inspired social, environmental, economic and military chivalry in other nations. With that said, I am not interested in riding cultural bandwagons of materialism, hate, or self-image idolatry. I love, enjoy and respect rigorous social scientific methods. Much chivalry can be found in the pursuit of truth, and creating technologies that improve lives. I do not, however, elevate the powers of human sciences over God. Finally, I love my faith the most. I do not, however, expect Christian theologies or leaders to be infallible. To better serve God, humans need to make spiritually chivalrous choices in their hearts each day; sometimes many times a day. No one can be expected to bat one thousand. Making the sincere effort is what God asks for.

(8)
Ennobled by God's Glory

Scientific and secular paradigms play invaluable roles in helping people to develop mental maps, resiliencies, knowledge, agency; countless skills for navigating physical and social worlds. On the other hand, healthy religious viewpoints offer the best resources for navigating the spiritual worlds. For centuries, billions of people have turned to faith to endure great hardships, survive extreme adversities and persevere chivalrously on their paths. World religions fill many human voids created or exacerbated by human cultures. Deepak Chopra pointed out that all religions incorporate doctrines of transcendence (spirit) and of the interconnectedness of all life (soul). Jesus Christ's mission on earth epitomised a world-revolutionising, spiritually chivalrous journey. Christ reopened human pathways to God's glory by dying for humankind's sins. In serving the poor, healing the wounded and freeing the captives, Christ blazed trails for others to reconnect with God.

Soren Kierkegaard, a 19th-century Danish philosopher, suggested that "knights of faith" can become ennobled by God. Using Abraham as an example, Kierkegaard suggested the life of a knight of faith involves facing series of internal and external hardships. Knights of faith journey spiritually. They choose to sacrifice cultural comforts and attachments to better serve God. They also stand strong in the face of opposition. Knights of faith let God guide their worldviews. They completely trust themselves and God, rather than one or the other. Journeys of Kierkegaard's knights of faith lead toward God, who ennobles their spirits for eternity through His glory.

Paradoxically, as knights of faith move beyond concerns with their own egos' glories and choose unselfishly to serve God and His higher glory, they may become spiritually glorified. The transformation of St Ignatius of Loyola exemplifies this. As a secular knight, he had sought and received social glory for his ego's prowess. Once bed bound, however, he began to contemplate a much higher source of glory and chivalry. St Ignatius experienced the dark night of the soul, spiritual yearnings and other processes identified by Joseph Campbell. Through his transformations he let go of his ego's desires for adulation. He became solely concerned with serving God. By serving God's glory without concern for his own, Ignatius became ennobled by God, venerated by humans as a saint.

Healthy religions guide inherently chivalrous spirits toward the ennoblement of God's glory. God's glory encompasses so many things, though, that it can be hard to define. Some version of the word glory appears in the Bible over 500 times. The Lord's Prayer ends with 'the glory forever...' Catholic Mass begins with the singing of 'Glory to God in the highest...' According to Myles Munroe, God's glory entails all that He is. God's glory is His perfect love, presence, character, mercy, chivalry, justice, peace, compassion, logic, etc. Munroe also proposes divine glory to be the true essence of all living things. Even in today's world, God's glory is never too far away. It is reflected in the eagle's flight and mastery, in the flower's full bloom. It can be evident in sunsets, landscapes, human altruism and virtues, chivalry, acts of love, the sounds of children's laughter, the mastery of skill, bravery and so forth. Persons may need to awaken the eyes of their hearts, however, in order to see it.

One of my favourite priests used to say, 'Human hearts were designed for Eden and Heaven.' Hearts were designed to connect with God's glory. John Eldredge discusses how "original glory" predated original sin in human hearts. Before the fall, God's presence filled Eden. His glorious ways were very visible to the first humans. Glory manifested in the love Adam and Eve shared, in their vocation of cultivating the Garden of Eden, the dominion they were given over plant and animal life, etc. Sins, of course, disrupted these arrangements. Adam and Eve's hearts became blocked from the connections their Creator designed them for. Christ, however, by dying for humankind's sins, paved new roads for human hearts to reestablish connections with God's glory. Today human hearts, however, need to journey to reconnect with glory. Jesus Christ gives a human face to a glory that would otherwise be impossible to see. The Holy Spirit comforts, counsels and guides those en route.

Many non-journeyers, however, try to fill their hearts with glory substitutes. Those who try to glorify their self-images, money, power, celebrities, social status, etc. may be attempting to meet deeper needs of their hearts' designs. Roads of idolatry, however, lead further away from God's glory. American culture often can be of poor guidance in these areas. The fast-moving, narcissistic currents of US culture today promote self-glorification as not only normal but desirable. A plethora of glory substitutes are readily available. Momentary ego-glorification may seem a text, "selfie", nose ring or video game victory away. It is worth noting that God's glory and social admiration can sometimes be compatible. If a journeyer is offered sincere admiration for his/her true noble qualities, then such admiration reinforces his/her spiritual paths. Spiritual journeyers, however, see social admiration as "bonuses". Connections with God and His glory are heart's true rewards.

God wants to ennoble inherently chivalrous, journeying spirits with His glory. Many spiritual qualities are ennobled through journeyers' following the Ten Commandments. Chivalry is certainly one of them. For example, the first Commandment asks followers to not put other gods before God. The idolatry involved would work against spiritual chivalry. Worshippers of idols would not receive the ennobling connections that God wishes for them. When people mention God's name vainly, such as to manipulate others into admiring their religiosity, they make idols of their false selves. By keeping the Sabbath day holy, journeyers set aside time each week to work on the inner journey of spiritual chivalry. In addition, it is spiritually chivalrous for children to honour their parents, especially when parents have sinned against them. These situations require much chivalrous forgiveness and inner work. Murdering, committing adultery, stealing, bearing false witness and coveting also harm the interests of spiritual chivalry.

Human spirits are inherently chivalrous. I have also argued that human spiritual chivalry can remain asleep or become misguided, serving the wrong causes and masters. Also, many people seek the false ennoblement of social admiration for chivalrous behaviours. These pursuits can result in "ego traps", stunting spiritual development. It is only through God that inherently chivalrous spirits can truly be ennobled. This only occurs under certain circumstances. As mentioned, persons have to choose the journey, to face internal and external gauntlets with spiritual graces and chivalry. Day after day, they have to keep choosing to follow their spiritual compass toward God. Since God wants to be able to ennoble chivalrous human spirits, though, He lends many kinds of assistance (discussed in chapter twelve).

Some debate exists over questions of whether or not believers can actually carry God's glory and ennoblement inside of them. Some Christians believe followers only access God's glory when directly connecting with the Spirit. God's glory stays completely with God. Others believe that advanced spirits become carriers of God's glory in some respects. For example, the Lutheran Doctrine of Imputation suggests Christ's righteousness is given to all followers through their faith. Believers carry God's righteousness, and therefore glory, inside of themselves. In my "and/both" opinion, both views can be true. What matters is where people are at in their noble journeys.

During initial spiritual awakenings believers enter into dependent relationships with the Father, Son and Holy Spirit. This phase of spiritual growth is similar to attachment stages that children experience with healthy mothers and/or fathers. For example, infants first form symbiotic attachments with parents. They experience their parents' love though direct connections. They cry when such connections are unavailable. If all goes well, children begin to separate from these attachments. Children of healthy parents take their experience of parental love with them as they separately explore their surroundings. In individuation stages, children become carriers of their parents' love. They access parental love within themselves even when not in direct contact with their parents. Of course, individuating children will still wish to reconnect with their parents directly throughout the day. But they also carry their parents' love inside of themselves.

Analogous stages seem to occur with journeyers' relationships with God. After early "attachment" stages of spiritual growth, journeyers move toward individuating from God to some degree. They begin to carry their experiences of connecting with God's glory inside of themselves even when not directly connecting with Him. Once God ennobles spiritual chivalry, journeyers become individuated carriers of His ennoblement. Naturally their hearts will seek renewed direct connections with Him. They are nonetheless able to access God's glory inside of themselves regardless. On the other hand, non-journeyers have not experienced individuation from God. They are unlikely to realise that one can be a carrier of God's glory. Their theological views will follow suit.

In the gospel of John, Christ states, 'The glory that you have given me I have given to them, that they may be one even as we are one,' (17:22). This passage suggests numerous aspects of God's honour, love, character, nobility, presence and nature are meant to be carried by journeyers. It also suggests that God's glory is meant to guide human-to-human bonds. Again, God asks followers to glorify Him for chivalrous reasons. He is unlike a narcissistic person, who cannot function without excessive admiration. God can stand alone with His glory. God asks followers to glorify Him for His followers' benefit. Giving glory to God moves followers past snares of idolatry. It also causes truly glorious qualities to increase inside of believers. Any aspect of God's character, nature and ways carried by followers magnifies when He is glorified. By glorifying God, journeyers experience more of His glory inside of themselves; more of God's glory flows through human relationships as well.

World religions are at their best when they guide inherently chivalrous spirits toward the ennoblement of God's glory. Not all churches hit this bull's eye. In my vast churchgoing experiences, I have encountered quite a few theologies of fear and control. Like the Pharisees, "hyper-conventional" congregations are so focused on conformity that they discourage spiritual chivalry. To be sure, members of these congregations can act very chivalrously when their egos want admiration. Yet their theologies foster ignoble divisiveness. Followers tend to bond through "us versus them" stances against others, rather than through healthier soul connections. Parishioners are taught that being Christian equals being extremely controllable. These churches seem to forget that Jesus Christ departed from many social conventions. Christ defied the oppressive power structures of his time. Jesus also advocated for loving one's enemies. His followers transcended artificial and unnecessary human divisions, becoming spiritually chivalrous.

Of course, the roots of these problems are not organised religion itself. I see churches as gifts from God. The deeper problem lies in what some non-journeyers do when they gain control of religious conventions. John Eldredge is acutely aware of these issues. He has authored numerous books designed to steer believers away from hyper-conventionality (in my words) and toward God. In *Wild at Heart,* Eldredge tackles negative impacts that hyper-conventional churches can have on men's souls. Eldredge argues that God intentionally designed a world full of beauty and danger. Danger can be evidenced by bears, sharks, lightning, disasters, but also wars and famines. And there are divine reasons for the world's dangers. They create opportunities for journeyers to develop courage, resilience, chivalry, faith, etc.

Eldredge proposes that male souls are designed by God to embrace these dangers in the right ways. He argues that the male soul inherently longs for adventures, battles and chivalrous deeds. In making his case, Eldredge emphasises that boys across world cultures play superhero and soldier. They are not simply acting out of testosterone or cultural conditioning. To Eldredge, their play expresses the inherent desires of their souls to embark upon noble and dangerous journeys. Eldredge is not, however, proposing a theology of "hyper-masculinity" as some may fear. Masculinity can indeed find life and chivalry in the presence of dangers. Eldredge argues that masculinity also flourishes through the offering of noble love, compassion and kindness. His view is "and/both".

Most boys do not fantasise about growing up to be "really nice guys", Eldredge adds. Nonetheless, many hyper-conventional churches try to force fit males into their nice guy moulds. When males sacrifice their souls' true longings (to chivalrously embrace dangers), in order to present themselves as really nice guys, fearful flocks are momentarily appeased. Disempowered males do not arouse contempt and envy among those who have forfeited their own souls' desires. Males who make these trade-offs, however, may be plagued by deep feelings that something is missing. Intense fear and rage can result from one's having been fooled into betraying his/her true soul's desires. Some males who act "super nice" in church act their rages out on their spouses and children behind closed doors. Similarly, some soul-wounded wives use religious dogmas to manipulate and exploit their husbands. Although these patterns are detrimental to spiritual chivalry, they can become normalised in some churches.

Fortunately, a sizeable number of churches lead congregates toward God. Again, churches and their leaders do not need to be perfect in order to do so. Christ's disciples definitely fell short of perfection. A healthy degree of spiritual chivalry, however, is needed for religious leaders to be effective in ways that matter the most. Many people can recite scripture. The best religious leaders draw experiences from their own noble journeys. While healthy religions include many conventional rituals and practises, they transcend them at the same time. On many occasions I have experienced a paradoxical blend of grounded connectedness (soul) and transcendence (spirit) during religious services. These churches fanned flames inside of me to continue my own spiritual journey; to support and honour this in others. I still think rationally throughout the day, but faith provides the over-arching perspective for my journey. One's journey with God can truly ennoble inherent spiritual chivalry.

(9)
Chivalry in Self and Social Control Systems

The noble character within advancing journeyers becomes more like that of God. Journeyers become more whole. Several aspects of holism have already been discussed. Resilience becomes more holistic. It blends inherently resilient qualities of awakened spirits and souls with attributes forged by navigating egos; as well as inborn qualities. Journeyers' worldviews become more comprehensive. Their integrated perspectives draw heavily from science, cultures and organised religions, while transcending biases and unnecessary divisions. Journeyers' personalities become more whole. Their awakened spirits and souls join forces through a shared sense of calling. This chapter adds social and self-control issues to the discussion. It will argue that the best self-control systems combine independent self-control resources with those gained from healthy interconnectedness—in ways conducive to spiritual and soulful chivalry.

When directed toward God, spiritual journeys led to chivalrous freedoms. It is not possible, however, for one to be truly free or chivalrous without possessing reasonable degrees of self-control. People who seek instantaneous feelings of freedom through drugs often end up enslaved by that which they thought has set them free. Addictions also offer a false sense of being in control of one's self. Many persons control their "Exiles" by self-medicating. But as drugs gain control over their personalities, self-control diminishes. While no human being has perfect self-control, many are noticeably deficient in it. A sizable number of Americans unjustly control others to compensate for their own deficiencies in self-control.

These patterns appear in high societal rates of bullying, violent crime, sex trafficking and domestic violence.

Potential ingredients of self-control can be many. Self-control includes being able to reign in one's emotions, arousal and impulses. Ability to delay gratification is also an aspect of self-control. Self-control also relates to perseverance and the resisting of temptation. It predicts resilience. Like resilience, self-control has a navigational component. Those with sufficient self-control are more adept at making choices, setting goals, taking steps toward them and disciplining themselves along the way. Other strengths, virtues and accomplishments are facilitated by self-control as well.

In Biblical terms, self-control is one of the "fruits of the spirit" (Galatians 5:22). Spirits graced with self-control are in better position to master the overall personality. The Bible acknowledges, though, that paths to self-control are not easy. Proverbs proposes that, 'He that rules his spirit is greater than he that taketh a city,' (16:32). It is a likely part of everyone's spiritual journey to struggle with self-control challenges. Scientific views can assist, however, by identifying patterned causes and effects of self-control. Many interesting models of self-control have emerged in recent years. This chapter will emphasise Schore's research. His work suggests that two different systems contribute to self-control. One system operates when people connect with others. The other functions more independent of human relationships. When these two systems operate more effectively and synergistically, self-control takes on new dimensions. Freedom and chivalry will follow. When this does not happen, social problems will likely result.

American culture has made control, but not self-control, something of a buzzword. Numerous products claim to help people "take control of their lives". Older men are advised to "take control of their hair loss" with hairpieces. A late-night "infomercial" informs me that I can take control of my finances with their programme. Perhaps "control" and "take control of your (fill in blank)" are marketable concepts because so many citizens experience a lack of personal control. In the information age, few shortages exist of situations that the average person may wish to have some control over. Much social angst is generated by economic uncertainty, terrorism, social and natural crises, family instability, etc. Anxiety lowers peoples' senses of control. Low sense of control increases anxiety. Many distressed persons gravitate toward addiction and/or unhealthy control dynamics with others. This distracts them from their anxiety, while offering a false sense of being in control of their minds, emotions and/or arousal. Dysfunctional practises backfire, however, and self-control shrinks further.

Self-control is more predictive of positive outcomes than self-esteem. Indeed, true self-esteem is an asset. In situations involving bullying, for example, the voice of true self-esteem can say, 'I don't deserve this.' On the other hand, when children are overly praised for mediocre work, self-control and humility suffer. Children high in self-esteem, yet low in self-control, lack the inner resources needed to sustain success. Many parents overly praised their children as substitutes for not developing healthy bonds with them. Healthy attachments are one of the best ways to build foundations for self-control. To deny legitimate bonding needs of children, while showering them with excessive praise, is to court self-control disasters. This is especially true when social anxiety is in the air. In contrast, children strong in self-control will arrive at healthy self-esteem. Their character and accomplishments will elicit positive feedback.

As mentioned, Schore's research suggests humans develop two different self-control systems. These are referred to as "interactive self-regulation" and "autoregulation". Systems of interactive self-regulation create self-control through human connections and relationships. "Autoregulation" operates more independently of relationships. Self-regulation refers to the management of emotions, impulses and states of brain arousal. The optimal levels of brain arousal exist in-between the extremes of being overly aroused, or not aroused enough, for the situation at hand. Hyper-arousal, being too mentally aroused, can appear as anxiety or mania. Hypo-arousal can relate to depression. Persons with healthy arousal-control systems live much of their lives in between hyper- and hypo-arousal. For simplicity's sake this book substitutes the term self-control for Schore's self-regulation and uses "independent self-control" for autoregulation.

Schore's model suggests that the best social foundations for self-control do not come from iron-fisted enforcements of social rules. They emerge instead from trusting bonds and connections. Social bonds are the seeds of healthy "interactive self-control". When persons connect with others in secure ways, they experience calming effects borne of love, trust and intimacy. True intimacy contributes to self-control. When people are calmly connected, they automatically gain a sense of control over their minds, emotions and arousals. It takes no great act of human willpower to control oneself during these moments. Healthy connections also provide anchors for people to process experiences of hyper- and hypo-arousal. Bonds give one something healthy to "come up to" or "come down from", allowing the brain to spend more time in optimal arousal ranges. Some people experience intimate bonds daily. Unfortunately, others only have vague notions of what secure bonds feel like. Those with attachment traumas, in particular, may not know they can gain self-control from human connections.

On the other hand, independent self-control systems can encompass a wide range of practises that permit persons to more autonomously regulate their brain arousals, impulses and emotions. Mindfulness, deep breathing, exercising, anger management and meditation are facilitators of independent self-control. Alone or in the company of others, healthy independent self-control systems help persons come down from hyper-arousal, rise up from hypo-arousal and to process related experiences. Athletics can be great teachers of self-control. Most athletes draw from a host of independent (and interactive) resources to harness their energies, manage emotional intensity levels, control their breathing, shift their mental approaches, adjust body positioning, etc. Popular American leisure activities are conducive to independent self-control as well. Jogging, fishing, gardening, playing musical instruments and numerous other activities help persons to gain relative control over their minds, bodies and/or emotions.

"Interactive self-control" and "independent self-control" are distinct yet overlapping systems. Both exist to some degree in most all persons. When functioning together, these systems create synergistic self-control resources. Most individuals and cultures, however, lean toward one system or the other. This seems especially true in times of stress or crisis. For example, individuals relying heavily upon independent self-control tend to push others away when distressed. This helps them regain a sense of being independently in control. Persons who have suffered attachment traumas may lean even further toward independent self-control. They perceive few bonding options.

In Criminology, Self-Control Theory proposes that childhood bonding difficulties can create self-control challenges that persist throughout persons' lives. Authors Hirschi and Gottfredson emphasise that low self-control is predictive of many criminal and analogous behaviours in childhood, adolescence and adulthood. Persons low in self-control are more likely to have long police records, serial relationships, poor employment records, drug/alcohol problems, etc. In many cases, childhood processes of attachment, separation and individuation from mother and father figures were disrupted by abuse, neglect, abandonment, etc. Parents were unable to offer healthy bonds to them. To survive these, children forged "insecure attachment styles". Persons with "avoidant" attachments, for example, try to connect in non-intimate ways. Insecure attachment styles afford some semblance of "bonding" while not facilitating the kinds of bonds conducive to calming, self-control, autonomy, joy, etc. Souls remain deprived.

Trauma recovery is part of many people's journeys. Attachment traumas are seen as the most difficult to overcome. Chapter fifteen will detail trauma recovery processes. It is worth noting here that most cope the best they can with the resources they possess at the moment. Children of dysfunction do try to control their own emotions, impulses and arousals. They may try to build independent self-control skills in emotional deserts without constructive parental role models. As juveniles, however, many decide that drugs/alcohol lend better self-control resources than dysfunctional bonds do. Drugs/alcohol may initially seem like miracle cures. Drugs/alcohol calm hyper-arousal and provide lifts from hypo-arousal in ways that unhealthy human connections cannot. To conventional psychiatric perspectives, though, these juveniles may need "meds". Powerful legal drugs can replace illegal ones. Juveniles' psychiatric symptoms may improve, but meds alone do not lead to interactive self-control. Interacting with healthy people does.

Noble journeys can nonetheless begin for attachment-wounded juveniles. Counselling may offer healthy bonding and mentoring opportunities that many childhoods lack. Still, it can be difficult to convince people with deep attachment trauma to open up to intimacy. Having not experienced healthy connections, they may not be able to see how dropping their guard and trusting a counsellor will lead anywhere safe, secure, or beneficial. Those courageous enough to trust, however, may learn that recovering from trauma significantly increases their self-control (among other things). Healing from intense fears, longings and rage drastically increases independent self-control. A therapeutic bond between counsellor and client lends itself to interactive self-control.

Healthy self-control can exist in paradoxical relationship with healthy self-surrender. Sometimes one must also lose control, for the right reasons, to gain better control. It is largely up to individuals to decide, wisely, when to surrender parts of themselves and when not to. Surrendering to trustworthy people can help build bonds and enhance interactive self-control. Surrendering to God blesses believers with spiritual graces and gifts. Typically, when one surrenders to God and healthy people, others come back stronger and more whole. On the other hand, when people surrender control to toxic human beings, and/or their own addictions or sins, they usually lose something in the process. It is important for journeyers to clarify what they can or cannot control. It is equally important that they learn who to surrender to and who not to. To improve discernment one may ask, 'When is it spiritually chivalrous to surrender, and when is it spiritually chivalrous not to?'

Attachment avoidance is not the only self-control issue plaguing Americans. Numerous citizens swing far in the opposite direction. Those with dependent attachment styles rely too heavily on human relationships for self-control. To overly-rely upon interactive self-control can cause some to struggle with being alone and/or standing on their own two feet. Some may mask their shortcomings behind personas of independence, especially in a culture which prizes self-reliance. Their self-control systems, however, may be too "co-dependent". These persons struggle to find independent resources for managing their emotions, impulses and states of arousal—outside of their relationships. Their noble journeys will include stepping toward healthy self-reliance, one day at a time. The different challenges involved in developing one's dual self-control systems are central to most any journey. The ideal blend of these two systems for a given individual, however, likely varies by his/her calling and social circumstances.

To my beliefs, God gives every animal, person and culture somewhat different self-control challenges and resources. With that said, God likely guides each journeyer to the blends of independent and interactive self-control that best suit his/her calling. This may also hold true for animals. Deepak Chopra suggests that seekers look to the animal Kingdom to glimpse the diversity of God's designs. Some species seem designed to need their packs, flocks, or herds to provide them with interactive self-control. Felines and birds of prey seem to navigate with high degrees of independent self-control.

A quick comparison of dogs and cats can be illuminative. By design, many canines rely upon interactive self-control. Their owners appreciate their attentiveness and loyalties. Yet some dogs are ill-equipped to control themselves when their owners are absent. Couches and blankets can get trashed. On the other hand, the self-control systems of cats seem to favour independent self-control. Our feral cat, Tally, prowls the night alone. She hunts with independent grace, intelligence and agility. My wife and I would like to see a little more of her. When Tally does surrender to us, she radiates a joy that comes from choosing to trust and bond. But Tally's independent self-control systems would sustain her if we weren't around.

Animals and humans both seem to follow their basic preferences, for independent or interactive self-control, when faced with threats and uncertainties. When our cats are startled, they run and hide somewhere by themselves. Dogs, on the other hand, often tenaciously stay by their owners' sides. Analogous phenomena can occur in human worlds. Cultures in crisis follow their general preferences toward interactive or independent self-control. Often the first instinct of individualistic cultures is to amplify the virtues of self-reliance (independent self-control). As America's Great Depression gripped the nation, Herbert Hoover gave his speech on the need for "rugged individualism". It soon became clear, however, that collective individualism alone would not solve these large-scale problems. Franklin Delano Roosevelt shifted to more collectivistic, New Deal policies. To survive the Depression and WWII, individualistic American culture implemented systemic strategies conducive to interactive self-control.

Similarly, overly collectivistic cultures can neglect the human spirit when over-emphasising interactive self-control. Even relatively balanced cultures can become split in times of crisis and transition. One cultural force promotes individualism; rival factions and promote collectivism. Post-WWII France is one example. Following the devastations of war, French culture split between two rival worldviews. One perspective, fuelled by the existentialist philosophy movement, asserted that it is up to individuals to master themselves and find their own meanings amid life's horrors. French existentialism held up individualism and independent self-control as solutions for collective trauma recovery. At the same time, Marxist structuralism had many post-war French adherents. This perspective asserted that France's social order will need to be reconstructed in ways that provide economic equality for all. Marxist solutions promoted collectivism and interactive self-control as cultural recovery mechanisms.

Of course, some parallels can be drawn between post-war France and the US today. American society has experienced a series of transitions and traumas; that is, over a decade of war, 9-11, natural disasters, major economic recession, terrorism, middle-class decline, the information age and the global economy. The former social order which birthed the 1950s American Dream has drastically changed. Political parties are divided by opposing worldviews (including views on what constitutes chivalry). American leftists tend to emphasise interactive self-control and collectivism. Liberal campaigns for universal health care, removing tax breaks for wealthy citizens and increasing opportunities for the poor, women, racial/ethnic minorities and sexual minorities, are collectivistic solutions to social traumas. In contrast, right-wing American solutions point to independent self-control and individualism. Conservative platforms tend to emphasise the protection of self-reliant individuals, families and businesses from excessive taxes and large government. They assert that hard-working, independent individuals can solve their own problems if freed from unjust governmental intrusions.

As with post-war France, valid points exist on both sides. When partisans cannot compromise, however, self-control systems, important individualistic and collectivistic values and even the spirit and the soul may become divided in a culture's consciousness. This also holds true for chivalry. Souls awaken chivalry when genuinely concerned with interconnectedness and ensuring others' welfare. Spirits awaken chivalry through more independent attempts to transcend circumstances and injustices. The best solutions for divisions on any level would include "and/both" thinking. Spirits and souls could both be valued. Individualism can blend with collectivism. Chivalry can thrive in spirit and soul domains.

Any path toward holistic self-control can be inherently painful and challenging. Cultural divisions, economic crises, technological changes and societal transitions add extra layers of challenge. Overuse of information technology in American has added self-control challenges. The average attention span for college students today is between 8 and 12 minutes. The bonding of many college students today is mediated by their cell phones and computer screens. Face-to-face connections, however, are much more conducive to interactive self-control. Meanwhile, many children's playgrounds for building independent self-control have shifted to indoor worlds of home entertainment. Such trends limit the kinds of independent resources that children and adults may develop. Online gambling, texting, social media, internet pornography and video games have become common substitutions for human interactions. Online addictions give people a false sense of being in control with their virtual worlds. These addictions, however, decrease their potentials for developing true self-control in the very world.

A sizable number of persons try to compensate for self-control deficiencies by controlling others in unjust, unhealthy and self-serving ways. As suggested, social indicators of this include high rates of bullying, sexual violence and domestic abuse. All are acts of power and control. Generally speaking, the more out of control that abusers feel, the more likely they will try to dominate, exploit, degrade and manipulate others to feel momentarily in control. Abuse victims, in turn, can habitually give up their power to appease controlling bosses, parents, spouses, etc. This may be their best survival option, but their self-control resources diminish as well. Controllers and controlees reinforce dysfunctional control dynamics. Controllers attempt to control themselves by controlling others. Controlees learn to control themselves by acclimating to others' unjust control over them. Neither pattern leads to holistic self-control.

Students sometimes ask me to clarify my views on disciplining children in light of my "and/both" views on control. I start by saying that very real differences exist between responsible parents who set needed limits on children and child abusers. In cases of abuse, discipline is driven by abusers' needs for control, rather than children's needs for healthy limits. Again, abusers feel out of control of their own emotions, impulses and arousals. The act of oppressing an animal, child, spouse, subordinate, etc. gives abusers momentary feelings of having control over something. Abusers' control is largely an illusion, though. They are usually highly deficient in interactive and independent self-control. Odds are their children will be as well.

In contrast, true discipline is driven by children's development needs. Children need some healthy limits and consequences in order to develop self-control. True internal freedom is not possible without a reasonable degree of self-control. Healthy discipline increases self-control in children, advancing their paths toward freedom, resilience, chivalry and so forth. Responsible parents discipline not because they are feeling out of control. They discipline out of noble love. They see consequences warranted by their children's actions or inactions. They also want their children to develop into responsible, free and noble adults.

When I set limits on college students, I view it as extending "surrogate self-control" to them. Seven years ago, circumstances dictated that I implement a "tough on texting" classroom policy. On occasion I have kicked "repeat offenders" out of my college classes. I do not enjoy doing so. I enforce this policy because I believe my roles as professor and elder warrant it. "Text addicted" students need some experiences with limits to move in the direction of healthier self-control. My consequences might offer such a step. When setting such limits, I extend some of my own self-control resources to students in need. It can be draining. But, again, these students are seriously lacking in their own self-control at those moments. I do not need to control their texting to feel in control of myself. Usually I have enough control over myself as is. Text addicted students, however, seem to need my surrogate self-control to control themselves.

How social control fits into my views on self-control is another common topic of classroom discussion. A number of different social forces are concerned with controlling citizens who are out of control; that is, police, prisons, psychiatry, etc. Social control is sometimes a social necessity. I have worked in positions that required me to physically restrain overly aggressive persons. Innocent people would have been hurt if I hadn't. But physical restraints alone never solved anyone's deeper self-control problems. To the contrary, some persons seemed to develop dependencies on being restrained in order to feel in control of their aggressions. I see social control as a sometimes-necessary means, rather than as an end. Better long-term outcomes occur when persons who once needed to be restrained develop self-control.

As another example, say that a dangerous, out-of-control drug offender is apprehended by law enforcement. Here, social control is in the interests of both the community and this individual. This hypothetical person enters a drug court programme. If treatment is effective, his/her self-control resources will increase. In this example, social control (police) served as a means to a person's developing more self-control (treatment). Indeed, it can be very chivalrous to risk one's body and life in order to intervene when people are out of control. Much chivalry can also emerge from painstaking efforts to help offenders develop self-control. If offenders choose to journey, to change habits and improve their self-control, they too become more chivalrous. When social control practises lead to self-control, many more people can become ennobled.

The US today is a world leader in prison rates. Incarceration addresses one issue related to out-of-control citizens. Communities are safer. For American control practises to be more effective, however, correctional systems would need to improve their provision of treatment and rehabilitation services. Some hardened inmates would decline treatment even if it was brought to them. Others, however, would choose it. Over time these persons could develop healthier self-control, resilience, coping resources, etc. Those gaining in self-control can journey to greater freedom, dignity and chivalry, impacting their worlds more positively. Effective prevention policies would yield even better outcomes. Self-control and resilience skills could be taught to many more at-risk youths, in the contexts of healthy mentoring bonds. If more citizens developed self-control, US society could spend less time, money and energy on social control.

With compasses set toward God, journeyers begin to master control and surrender. Their independent and interactive self-control systems both develop, regardless of their culture's leanings. Independent self-control allows for more mastery of one's self. This enhances freedom and noble spiritual virtues. Interactive self-control enables the soul to bond more maturely and meaningfully with others. Healthy bonds facilitate compassion, empathy, love and chivalry of the soul. Journeyers become more independent and inter-dependent at the same time. They are able to chivalrously offer much more gifts and resources to their surrounding worlds.

(10)
Chivalry vs. American Narcissism

Another way to shed light on spiritual chivalry is to discuss where it is lacking. The next two chapters focus on common American trends toward narcissism and dogmatism. To be sure, narcissists and dogmatists can engage in chivalrous behaviours. Narcissists may project chivalrous images of themselves if this yields social admiration. Dogmatists may behave chivalrously for groups their egos need to attach with to feel secure. Yet the spirits and souls of the pathologically narcissistic and dogmatic slumber. When existent, their chivalrous behaviours are not related to spiritual journeys leading toward God's glory.

In American culture, narcissism increased significantly with the millennial generation. Twenge and Campbell found that 9% of millennial college students met criteria for narcissistic traits. This spiked from 2% of previous generations. Among other things, pathological narcissists make idols out of their own self-images. They are trapped in their egos or false selves. Narcissist may degrade, abuse and exploit many people in their efforts to keep their false selves elevated over others. In many respects, US culture has normalised self-image idolatry. Narcissism appears natural and even desirable to many Americans. Yet as narcissism increases in a culture, true chivalry diminishes.

Assuredly every person develops some kind of false self. Carl Jung suggested that human personas are archetypal. Everyone has an inborn "mask". And in some circumstances, life would be hard to navigate without one. When narcissism is extreme, however, the false self never leaves the helm of the personality. At the helm, the narcissistic Protector Part does little to dialogue with other parts of the personality. The personality is reduced to little more than a set of well-crafted images and projections. Healthier persons can have personas that take the steering wheel in certain situations. Job interviews are one example. Once these situations end, however, other personality parts resume control.

Some developmental theories see "primary narcissism" as a normal aspect of childhood development. Children raised in healthy environments simply grow out of their egocentricity. They replace it with something better. Pathological narcissists, however, do not. This chapter focuses on the pathological end of the narcissism continuum. Trends in American narcissism warrant discussion for a number of reasons. American journeyers need heightened abilities to discern healthy from unhealthy narcissism—amid a culture that glorifies it. Also, when journeyers better recognise patterns of narcissism, they are better able to respond with spiritual graces. Spiritual journeyers themselves need to transition from being led by their false selves to spiritual leadership. Finally, cultural narcissism negates spiritual chivalry. American culture cannot move in spiritually chivalrous directions without getting a better handle on self-image idolatry.

Pathological narcissism actually resembles an addiction. Narcissists are addicted to the admiring attention that lavishes their false selves. Like alcohol to alcoholics, narcissists intensely crave admiring attention for the self-images they present. They seem to believe that if they exploited enough peoples' admiration, their false selves would transform into something true. Like other addicts, narcissists experience emptiness and withdrawal when removed from their "drug" of social admiration. No amount of admiration will truly satiate them. Admiration is survival necessity. Their false selves would likely crumble without the social adulation that props them up. Few other personality parts could take the steering wheel should the false-self fail. Their spirits and/or souls have not awakened.

Several cultural currents are particularly conducive to narcissism. For example, some channels of American individualism promote "doing your own thing" over virtues of sacrificing for others. Narcissists can become glorified icons of these strands of individualism. The American Dream linked success and social glory to money and material possessions.

Narcissists are highly skilled at manipulating social status. The self-esteem movement lost sight of differences between narcissism and true self-esteem. Narcissists score very high on self-esteem measures. American marketing promotes statements such as "image sells" and "image is everything". This too speaks to narcissists' languages. Narcissistic trends have led American culture adrift from humility. This also gives licence to narcissists. Seeing oneself realistically could equal death of the false self. The false self's existence is sustained by untruths and partial truths.

All narcissists seem to truly believe is that they are superior to others. Many hide their haughtiness behind deceptive masks, however, including ones of false humility. In subtle yet calculated ways, narcissists exalt their "superior" qualities above the gifts, virtues and chivalries of those around them. Narcissistic Protector Parts see it as fact that they are more admirable than others. What narcissists believe makes them superior, though, can vary person to person. Some believe that having a perfect body elevates their worth. For others superiority stems from their superior intellect, winning self-image, even unquestionable ethics. Narcissists can be hostile and sometimes violent toward those who appear to threaten the sources of their superiority. They believe they would obliterate without their false selves. Again, they do not know that they can awaken their spirits and souls. Consequently, they protect the superiority of their false selves with a "life or death" intensity. Narcissistic parents are capable of doing great destruction to their own children to preserve their self-images. Less violent ones ensure that their self-image comes before their children's needs.

Narcissists project the image of being virtually free from stresses and problems. This is designed to manipulate people into admiring them as superior. Narcissists do, however, experience some of the stressors and crises that other people do; though they are not prone to experiencing others' pain. Narcissists worry obsessively about their own self-image. Amid significant social change, narcissists can feel lost. When this occurs, narcissists will try to make changing environments fit their pre-existing mental maps. Their mental maps highlight ways they are superior to others; entitling them to social admiration and glory. During transition, narcissists may seek new ways of manipulating admiration for false selves. They do not typically change their core beliefs regarding their own superiority, though.

Narcissists skilfully alter their personas to fit different situations. They find cunning ways of manipulating social admiration across a wide gamut of social events. Because of their innate superiority, narcissists feel entitled to be seen as celebrities. Narcissists cleverly seize celebrity status at other peoples' weddings, graduations, celebrations, retirement parties, etc. A narcissist may, for example, solicit admiration at someone else's event by being so wonderful as to attend. Toward securing social admiration narcissists think win/lose. They think, 'I am the centre of social glory so you cannot be.' Narcissists become victims of their own success. They are so good at manipulating admiration and maintaining the personality's steering wheel, that their essential qualities of self do not awaken. Filled with idolatry, their hearts remain starved for true connection.

It is worth emphasising that healthier people also don personas and can even promote themselves, in certain contexts. Those who self-present well in job interviews increase their odds of being hired. Situational use of false selves does not automatically signal narcissism or its pathology. When I teach auditorium classes, my own self-image helps me to maintain my boundaries, mental focus and sense of identity. My persona also gives my students, who will not truly know me as a person, some consistent sense of who I am. I do, however, work to ensure that my classroom persona reflects truths of who I am on the inside. When these lectures are over, I am very ready to remove the persona. In contrast, masks stay in place for pathological narcissists. They may shrewdly change their outward appearances to fit different situations, but an underlying mask is always there. Narcissists believe that personas are who people really are.

In some respects, narcissists can appear resilient. Narcissistic persons persevere toward their self-image goals without letting others' needs stand in their way. Their resilience, however, is completely tied to their personas. The narcissistic version of "flexibility" involves a chameleon-like altering of personas in order to seize admiration in different social environments. Underneath the mask, narcissists' superiority beliefs are highly inflexible. Narcissists can be very strong-willed in their efforts to keep their false selves glorified. Yet they lack a will to grow, change, love, serve, etc. Narcissists can utter empathic words that may sound convincing, but they are only spoken to solicit admiring attention. True empathy has nobler intentions to it. Narcissists' resilience begins and ends with their intense desires to keep their personas elevated. Their false selves are the very linchpins of their personalities.

Personas of narcissists can, however, be great barometers for what a given culture values at a certain point in time. Narcissists find ways of becoming the self-images that garner the most admiration in any group or culture. American culture strongly values self-reliance. Many American narcissists project images of being "independent", "autonomous" and "in control of their lives". Yet narcissists are none of these in any true sense. If persons are highly dependent upon others to admire them as independent people, they are not truly independent. Narcissistic people are more in control of their personas than they are of their own minds, emotions, wills and lives. Underneath façades of being in control, narcissists are actually very controlled by admiration addiction. The interactive self-control of narcissists is devoid of true love, trust, calm and intimacy. Meanwhile the independent self-control of narcissists is not directed toward chivalrous freedom.

In his book *Evil*, Roy Baumeister identifies narcissism in Lucifer's fall from Heaven. The archangel Lucifer wanted to be worshipped. Although many gifts were bestowed upon him, Lucifer became unwilling to serve God. Instead he wanted his false glory to be elevated above God's true glory. Consequently, Lucifer and the rebellious angels were cast out of Heaven. On earth Lucifer could extort what he truly wanted. He could manipulate some human beings into glorifying him as a god, even though he is not. Many theologians have discussed Lucifer's sinful pride. His story is one of narcissism. Lucifer chose to try to exalt his false self over healthier connection with God. Of course, Baumeister is not suggesting that all narcissistic persons are evil. Many narcissists are simply immature. But pathological narcissism will likely be found in any place that evil exists.

The Greek myth of Narcissus and Echo is also illuminative. Echo was a nymph who fell in love with the handsome Narcissus. She wanted to be his companion. In his haughtiness, however, Narcissus showed contempt for those who truly loved him. His truest love was his own self-image. When Narcissus saw his own reflection in a lake, he fell so in love with it that he perished. Like Lucifer, Narcissus was not interested in true connections or intimacies that nurtured his soul. He ditched Echo. When Narcissus lost Echo, he lost his soul's companion. On a more symbolic level, an "echo" symbolises the reverberation of one's voice. When Narcissus lost Echo, he symbolically lost the voice of his true self as well. This symbolism gets to the core of pathological narcissism. Narcissistic persons become so enraptured by their own self-images that they lose healthy interconnectedness; and the inner voices of their spirits and souls.

Some debate exists as to where pathological narcissism comes from. Some believe that it stems from childhood traumas and deprivations. Others believe that narcissism is more inherent. Both could be true. Many narcissists experience childhood attachment traumas. Poor bonding options impede one's ability to developing concerns for others, as well as self-control. It may make some sense for a child's narcissistic Protector Part to stay at the helm when abuse is omnipresent; when healthy connections are unavailable. On the other hand, narcissists can also grow up with doting mothers and/or fathers. This attention, however, is not offered unconditionally. These parents overly-praise their children's successes and appearances, while depriving them of healthy connections for their true feelings, thoughts and inner worlds. Young narcissists consistently receive the message that "only appearances of success matter". The larger culture, in turn, may reinforce this belief.

An interesting interpretation of inherent narcissism is offered by Robert L. Moore. He proposed that everyone has inherent grandiosity in him/her. Inherent grandiosity comes from our intuitive knowledge that we possess a spark of God within us. While childhood traumas may make it harder to control inherent grandiosity, they are not the root causes of it. Moore referred to this inherent grandiosity as the "dragon". Addicts, including narcissists, can be consumed by their own dragons (grandiosities). Mania results from persons getting too close to the energies of their own dragons. In Western traditions, dragons are depicted as destructive creatures that need to be slain. These myths communicate the message that inherent grandiosities need to be dominated.

Other cultural traditions depicted dragons as formidable forces for good. These myths symbolically suggest that inherent grandiosity can be harnessed to serve higher purposes. Moore agrees, proposing that persons need to learn to contain their dragon energies. This meshes with views of Robert Wicks and the Zen masters he quotes. They argue that persons can learn to "ride" their dragons. Our sense that we have a spark of God within us could drive us to great heights of noble love, courage and sacrifice. To ride the dragon would be to use our "dragon energies" for spiritually chivalrous purposes. On the other hand, when persons' inherent grandiosities drive their personalities, many problems ensue. This is the case for pathological narcissists.

Richard Rohr has written extensively on differences between the true self and the false self. Rohr argues that four major "splits" from reality facilitate false selves. The first entails persons splitting from their "shadow" sides, their unwanted personality parts and pretending to be their idealised selves. The second occurs when people split their minds from their bodies and souls—then live solely in their minds. The third involves splitting life from death, trying to live without the concept of "death". The fourth appears when persons split themselves from other people. They try to live apart, superior and separate from others. Any human being can make these splits. Some cultures, however, normalise them.

John Eldredge asserts that the spiritual journey begins when the false self fails. In pre-journey stages of life, it is normal for persons to hide their wounds behind false selves. False selves are Protector Parts. They protect us from being re-wounded in the same places. As mentioned, noble journeys are often initiated by crisis. These crises re-wound persons in the places that their false selves have been working overtime to protect.

Combinations of life crises and failures of the false self are telltale signs that one's journey is beginning. Persons experiencing these situations have fateful choices to make. They can proceed on paths of falsehood by repairing or re-inventing their false selves. They can instead choose to journey into the unknown with uncertain mental maps.

The perspectives of Moore, Rohr, Eldredge and others suggest that anyone in any culture could become narcissistic. American culture, however, sets up conditions particularly suited for narcissism. The social contract has diminished, and economic insecurities foster extremely competitive climates. Many people in cutthroat situations may not wish to lose their false selves. In addition, overworked families fall short of the quality time needed for secure bonds to develop. Overly stressed parents may offer excessive praise as substitutes for deeper connections. Children can feel entitled to this. High levels of entitlement, plus low levels of healthy bonding, can forge very tenacious false selves. Narcissism has increased at a faster rate for females. The popular culture's barrage of beauty images may account for some increases by gender. Many girls are taught that they must look like a model in a magazine to have any social value. Meanwhile information technology has brought reductions in the face-to-face interactions that could otherwise generate empathy. Lack of empathy is a defining characteristic of pathological narcissism.

It is worth noting that information technology did not create the narcissism epidemic. It has, however, poured gasoline on the fire. Social media allows narcissists 24/7 access to "narcissistic supply". According to Vaknin, "narcissistic supply" refers to the persons that narcissists use as their admiration "stash". Narcissists keep many "friends" in reserve, ready at the drop of a hat to admire their false selves. Information technology allows narcissists to have immediate access to their pools of admirers most any time day or night. If a narcissist is running low on admiring attention at 11:00 p.m. (and fearing the crumbling of his/her false self), he/she can simply log on to social media. It is likely that one of his/her 500 friends will offer admiration for his/her new posting. The narcissist's fears are assuaged for a few minutes. For narcissists to have social media accounts is akin to alcoholics living in back rooms of liquor stores. "Fixes" are always available. The odds that a given narcissist will ever "bottom out", seek help and begin a spiritual journey assuredly decrease.

In counselling fields, narcissistic personality disorder is regarded as difficult but not impossible to treat. For one thing, most narcissistic clients quickly learn to "talk the talk" of therapy. Many try to manipulate counsellors into admiring them as "superior clients". Also, narcissists experience extreme anxieties over the thought of removing their masks. It is similar to an alcoholic's fear of withdrawal. Like other addicts, narcissists need very compelling reasons to shed their personas, walk away from "narcissistic supply" and step into the unknown. They may need to hit bottom to find such compelling reasons. An alcoholic in early recovery typically avoids bars, liquor stores and the aisles in grocery stores that contain alcohol. Analogously, recovering narcissists should cancel social media and avoid people who might otherwise admire their false selves.

Chapter fourteen will discuss how Internal Family Systems theory can help people to transform problematic Protector Parts. It is certainly possible for spirits and souls to awaken amid the ashes of narcissism. One step at a time, recovering narcissists may awaken true emotions and thoughts. Astute counsellors will offer consistent and respectful connections, while avoiding admiring their clients' personas. Therapeutic bonds can begin to create interactive self-control. Clients' longing for connections with God and their true selves can be ignited. Piece by piece, a recovering narcissist and skilled counsellor pull forth a true self. Still, any narcissist in recovery today is tormented by the knowledge that "narcissistic supply" is only a simple click or a text away.

Encounters with narcissism will be a part of most everyone's spiritual journey, though some more than others. Journeyers fare better by keeping their compasses set on God and seeking opportunities amid the danger. Narcissists actually provide opportunities for strengthening one's resolve, gaining better control over feelings, discerning truths from falsehoods, etc. The ability to detect patterns of narcissism improves journeyers' strategies and resources. Many potential pitfalls can be avoided.

I cannot completely avoid contact with narcissists on a college campus. When I see a narcissist approaching me, however, I immediately consider his/her agenda. No matter the ruse, this person will want me to do something to admire his/her false self. Mindful of this I raise my guard, preparing to filter through smokescreens and choose my best response. I listen with a basic respect, but don't let this person's agenda violate my mind. I know that if I don't give admiration, I may not be approached by this narcissist again. At times I feel sorry for narcissists. They spend so much energy trying to gain social glory for their false selves. They comprehend so little of true glory. Underneath the mask they are very lonely and frightened.

Rates of narcissistic traits among college students have slightly declined with the transition from Millennials to iGens. Narcissism thrives in the larger culture, but I encounter a little less of it in my classes than ten years ago. Decreases in narcissism, however, do not automatically mean a decline in idolatry. Many iGens seem idolatrous in slightly different ways. The stereotypical Millennial made an idol out of his/her esteemed self-image and then expected teachers to praise him/her for it. Thankfully the iGens are less "in your face" with their self-esteem. Many iGeners do seem idolatrous, though, toward that which makes them feel safe and validated; that is, their smartphones and social media accounts. Cultural trends change, but the need for human hearts to choose between idolatry and spiritual chivalry does not. Spiritual journeyers, however, are not chained to unhealthy trends of their surrounding cultures. With compasses set toward God, they advance toward spirit and soul chivalry even when culture might otherwise negate it.

(11)

Chivalry vs. American Dogmatism

Like narcissism, dogmatism is a common Protector Part that can be fuelled by idolatry. Narcissists create idols out of their self-images. Dogmatists embrace the idols of their social groups, countries, faiths, political parties and worldviews. Unlike narcissists, dogmatists are not addicted to admiring attention. They do, however, need to attach their minds to very rigid belief systems to hold their identities together. Whereas the false self is the linchpin of narcissistic personalities, rigid worldviews serve similar purposes for dogmatic people. Many dogmatists present chivalrous personas. They may sacrifice impressively for groups and beliefs they attach to. The idolatry impacting their hearts' choices, however, works against true spiritual chivalry.

Dogmatic Protector Parts are resistant to worldview changes. Dogmatists will go to great lengths to not revise outdated mental maps. To be sure, most everyone has Protector Parts that know how to steel their hearts and minds. Situational personality rigidity can be particularly useful in times of stress. It is also desirable to be firm in one's convictions. With dogmatism, however, rigid Protector Parts refuse to let go of the steering wheel. Many other important parts of the personality are then neglected. Voices of the spirit and soul are ignored. Unfortunately, some aspects of American culture have normalised and even glorified this phenomenon. Consequently, many Americans confuse pathological dogmatism with strength of character.

A dogmatists' rigid worldview could be religious, cultural, countercultural, political, scientific, etc. in nature. Dogmatists all seem to share an intense drive to maintain feelings of security. Their Protector Parts believe that permanent states of security will come from attaching to unbendable worldviews and groups. Dogmatists are quick to dismiss flaws in their worldviews (which might otherwise cause exiled insecurities to surface). Dogmatists can also be quick to disdain differences of opinion; that is, unless they are dogmatic about others' rights to have different opinions. Pathological dogmatists cannot let go of their rigidity without risking personality disorganisation and overwhelming feelings of insecurity. What prevents them from being flooded by insecurities, though, also impedes spirit and soul development.

Dogmatism increases in times of high cultural fears, stressors and transition. It can emerge as a "stage 3" strategy for feeling lost. Again, persons at stage 3 try to force-fit new realities into outdated mental maps. Dogmatic Americans concerned with the national economy, for example, may attach to inflexible views asserting that the American Dream is not in jeopardy. Not revising their mental maps permits dogmatists to stay rigid, not change and continue to feel in control of their inner turmoil. It is worth noting that many persons have both narcissistic and dogmatic Protector Parts. The narcissistic streak in dogmatists allows them to attach to idols of whole families, social groups and cultures. Narcissists, in turn, cling dogmatically to their beliefs in their own superiority.

Dogmatists tend to restrict their social circles to those who share their rigid beliefs. This allows them to avoid evidence that could challenge their views and evoke anxiety. Their coping strategies, however, come at costs. Their emotional rigidity hinders the development of truer intimacy and "interactive self-control". Emotions that are too shut down, or tightly regimented, are not open to healthy connections with others. Dogmatists' shackles of rigidity also stifle their independent self-control. Again, their spirits are not usually awakened, ennobled, or free.

Internal chaos, if not dealt with in healthier ways, eventually resurfaces. When this happens, dogmatists can display strong tendencies to scapegoat others. Many dogmatists believe that not being under their group's rigid control equals not being moral or worthy. These assumptions justify their lashing out at persons not equally dominated by their group's belief systems. A common defence mechanism for dogmatists involves projecting their own shortcomings onto others, then attacking those persons for what they appear to represent. Scapegoats may or may not actually possess the negative qualities that dogmatists project onto them. Acts of targeting scapegoats allow dogmatists to discharge unwanted emotions, restore rigidity, maintain some kind of self-control, defend their worldviews, "connect" with like-minded others and maintain illusions of security.

Dogmatists want their social group's belief systems to become a dominant and unquestionable reality. They believe that their minds can then attach to something unshakably secure. In the interests of advancing their group's agendas, dogmatists can be very willing to sacrifice themselves. Their sacrifices, however, differ from those of the spiritually chivalrous. Dogmatic Protector Parts sacrifice for the social group in order to keep deeper fears at bay. Their martyrdom is a defence mechanism. Their chivalrous behaviours are driven by fears. In contrast, spiritually chivalrous persons choose to sacrifice out of higher love. Their freedom allows them to be fully aware of their options. To choose to sacrifice, from a position of freedom, makes martyrdom nobler.

When I first taught college, I naively believed that educating students with important social scientific findings would automatically translate into important changes in their lives. This can indeed be true for some students. However, a number of young adults arrive at college with rigid worldviews firmly in place. Some are simply trying to please their parents by adopting their views. Others already need rigidity to hold their personalities together. The latter are especially prone to reject information that does not support their worldviews. Understanding dogmatism, however, has helped me to comprehend their internal dilemmas. Sometimes social scientific evidence exposes students to potential errors in their mental maps. This prompts them to either grow or reject the data. When a rigid system of beliefs is what holds a person together, the sheer thought of changing perspectives could open floodgates of distress. Dogmatic people do not believe they have anything to "fall back" upon. They see their best option as dismissing the evidence; along with opportunities to learn and grow.

Longshoreman philosopher Eric Hoffer's *The True Believer* still stands as a poignant inquiry into dogmatism. Hoffer wrote during the American "Red Scare". He used the term 'true believer' to describe political and religious dogmatists. To Hoffer, true believers cling to dogmas in order to evade responsibility for unwanted parts of their personalities. A true believer could be a devout fascist one decade and a committed communist the next. The actual political ideology mattered less. True believers need to affix their fragile minds to a dogma. What matters most to them is to secure social value within dogmatic groups. Hoffer saw true believers as dangerous to America's noble ideals. They may be extremely religious or patriotic, but true believers have bitter contempt for paths that truly set people free.

Recent fears, crises and transitions in the US have chequered its social landscape with dogmatism. True believers today are abundant in modern political spheres. US Congress is particularly divided. Dogmatic representatives of one party regularly lash out at the opposing party's dogmatists. While holding conflicting worldviews, political extremists are actually kindred in their underlying needs for dogmas. As mentioned, the American Dream lost much of its power to bridge political parties. Today's partisans hold their in-groups together with divisive ideologies that conflict with their rivals' divisive views. Many American voters mistake political dogmatism for character strength and convictions. Candidates who think "and/both" are at a disadvantage.

Different strands of dogmatism are alive and well in academia. A number of professors devote their careers to force fitting data into one rigid paradigm. Any evidence that does not fit these particular "boxes" is quickly discounted. Many fight pretty hard to ensure that their dogmas prevail. Dogmatists on the other side of intellectual fences fight equally hard. Academic dogmatists use scholarship to reinforce the rigid belief systems that hold their personalities together. They can form very exclusive groups. Like their political counterparts, academic dogmatists' bond through "groupthink". Dogmatists also rise to positions of influence in the academic world. Fortunately, many colleges also employ critical numbers of journeying professors who seek truths beyond dogmatism.

Academic dogmatism can be contrasted with concomitant currents of "anti-intellectual" dogmatism. Anti-intellectuals bond over mutual contempt for scientific evidence, intellectual refinement and the "educated elite". To be sure, spiritual journeyers do not have to possess Ph.D.'s or be college educated. They do, however, need to develop healthy respect for the human mind, heart and will to progress on one's spiritual paths. Many Reality T.V. shows espouse anti-intellectual worldviews. Anti-intellectualism is also a key ingredient in some religious movements. Dogmatic faiths usually depict a punitive God. These views facilitate personality rigidity. Dogmatic believers hope to permanently attach to a rigid God and feel secure forever. God, however, might have a different plan for them.

In general, anti-intellectualism rises when cultures swing too far to the political right or the left. For example, many men of knowledge were once forced to flee Nazi Germany. Professors in Communist China were shipped to pastures. Chris Hedges argues that professors emerge as threats to some political extremists because they possess means to expose cultural lies. Nazi lies of superiority claimed to restore Germany to mythical glory. Communist China boasted that equality enforced by violence would lead to a utopian society. When such cultural lies are spreading, competent professors can offer strong evidence to the contrary. Indeed, professors share human imperfections. The good ones, however, competently use theories, methods and mental resources to detect falsehoods, unveil truths, diagnose problems and suggest intelligent solutions. In the US today, a dominant lie fuelling anti-intellectualism is that the American Dream is not declining. By disrespecting scholars, anti-intellectual dogmatists attempt to delete evidence that might otherwise distress them.

Dogmatism also appears today in a wide assortment of hate groups. In America today, most anyone could potentially be hated by some group for who they represent. Acts of racism, terrorism, anti-policing, misogyny, misandry and homophobia are regular events. Hate and contempt are actually key ingredients to dogmatism. These emotions harden. They feed rigidity of cognition and emotion. It is worth noting that contempt itself can be a functional emotion. To feel contempt in the presence of human evil is not only normal, it is desirable. Contempt can help create boundaries, protecting souls from being too vulnerable. On the other hand, to consistently generate contemptuous feelings for good human beings who are simply different furthers social pathology.

Societal increases in narcissism and dogmatism are problematic not only in the toxicity they spread, but in the virtues they negate. The virtue of reverence is seen as an antonym of contempt. Dating back to ancient Greece and China, reverence has been viewed as a building block of civilisation. In the twentieth-century, Albert Schweitzer argued that "reverence for life" is a virtue that makes all other ethics and virtues possible. Dogmatists, however, lack reverence for spiritually chivalrous persons, views and paths. Spiritually awakened people cannot be easily controlled by their groups or worldviews. They do not need rigidity to hold their personalities together. If dogmatists possess reverence, it is for the idols of their social groups and/or worldviews. Reverence entangled with idolatry loses virtuousness. A general awakening of spirit/soul reverence in the US, however, could provide an antidote to toxic levels of contempt.

Chapter nine mentioned that the US is a world leader in prison rates. Unfortunately, the nation holds a similar dubious status for mental illness rates. Much fear and anxiety are in the air. Narcissists and dogmatists are among those inflicting abuses. Human hearts are not receiving healthy connections. Americans seeking mental health treatment, however, may not escape the nets of dogmatism. In European countries, mental illness is typically viewed as temporary, stress-induced and recoverable. In contrast, dogmatic American views assert that the same symptoms are biologically based and chronic. Dogmatic psychiatrists are quick to inform patients that they will need to take addictive medications for the rest of their lives. An "and/both" perspective might instead suggest that clients can take "meds" if helpful, while also receiving counselling for coping skills, self-control, resilience and/or trauma recovery.

True spiritual chivalry can seem extremely threatening to dogmatists, especially those who believe their groups hold monopolies on chivalry. By recognising important patterns of dogmatism, however, journeyers are less likely to be caught off guard. They will be able to choose their coping strategies in advance. In fair weather, dogmatists may seem less problematic than narcissists. They seem to embody normalcy. Dogmatists' willingness to sacrifice might even cast them in a refreshing light; as antidotes to excessive individualism. Yet fearful dogmatists can be as violent as pathological narcissists. Dogmatists have not developed healthy self-control systems. They need to be controlled by their social groups to hold themselves together. Fearing oblivion without their groups' control, most dogmatists will defend their views against all perceived threats. If paranoia sets in, more and more different "categories" of people will be designated as threats.

Rigid worldviews have no choice but to eventually crumble. They are built upon falsehoods. Nonetheless, countless dogmatists work overtime to try to prevent this from occurring. A dogmatic personality facing a collapse of worldview, and therefore inner security, would be expected to fragment further. This, however, could simply be a new beginning. His/her noble journey could start. God can provide recovering dogmatists (and narcissists) with far better versions of everything their "egos" so strongly desire. For example, dogmatic Protector Parts try hard to forge personality firmness by rigidifying hearts and minds. This firmness, however, comes at a great cost to their spirit and soul lives. On God's paths, journeyers become ennobled with "spiritual firmness". God's firmness unites all other parts of human personalities. Also, dogmatic egos seek security at all costs. The security gained through God, though, is truly ennobling and liberating.

Spiritual journeyers can find many opportunities amid dangers of rampant dogmatism. My frequent encounters with dogmatists have helped me develop more resilience, cunning, self-control, patience, mercy, compassion, etc. Dogmatists have also compelled me to stand up for scapegoats and/or higher truths, increasing my convictions. My need to respond to spiritually violent dogmatists and narcissists has given me opportunities to use God's armour. Ephesians (6:10-18) describes how donning God's belt of truth, breastplate of righteousness, sandals of peace, shield of faith and helmet of salvation enables a person to stand firmly and chivalrously against lies and assaults. God also provides one offensive weapon. This is the sword of the Spirit, God's word. I have spiritually violent dogmatists to thank for my even knowing that God offers spiritual armour to His journeyers. If encounters with narcissists and dogmatists prompt journeyers to be even more spiritually chivalrous, it's a victory for God's glory.

(12)

Spiritual Gifts and Leadership

Numerous blessings, gifts, strengths and virtues come out of spiritual journeys. Indeed, salvation is the ultimate gift. With that said, holistic resilience and self-control are substantial benefits as well. They make possible the gift of freedom. Journeyers' hearts are blessed with the connections with God they were designed for. Souls are gifted with deep and meaningful human relationships. Journeyers' spirits are ennobled with powers of self-leadership and self-mastery. The gift of calling helps spiritual and soulful purposes coalesce. Spiritual journeyers are further blessed with many more moments of inner calm, peace and joy. All Godly gifts, strengths and blessings are conducive to spiritual chivalry.

In chapter five I discussed transformational processes common to spirits, souls and egos. Converted spirits assume leadership of the overall self, egos become advisors and souls build meaningful connections while governing impulses and instincts. Among additional processes, shadow personality parts are reconciled (next chapter), while wounds become relatively healed (chapter fourteen). Again, God seems very willing to "co-pilot" these challenging processes. And every noble transformation is somewhat unique and universal at the same time. Unique are the distinct sets of strengths, trials and triumphs and soul relationships that each journeyer develops. More universal are the general roles that transforming spirits, souls and egos assume.

This chapter elaborates further upon spiritual gifts, leadership and identities. It describes additional gifts that advanced journeyers may receive, such as "ontological security" and "individualised divine consciousness". It also discusses some of the benefits of journeyers' discovering and embracing their spiritual identities. It is worth noting, though, that qualities of spirit can remain somewhat mysterious even to journeyers. Advanced journeyers may not fully grasp their spiritual capabilities and purposes. With compasses set toward God, however, they grasp enough of their spiritual qualities and potentials to meet the challenges of their callings.

One of my favourite examples of spiritual identity work comes from my wife, Tania. A few years ago, Tania was going through a series of career and personal transitions. At times she felt somewhat lost in her sense of identity. One day, for a change of scenery, I suggested that we take a drive around town and try an experiment. Tania agreed. As I drove around, I asked Tania to be mindful of what she notices in the people, cars, houses, etc. that we pass by. She began to vocalise her observations to me. It soon became clear that Tania's mind really zeroes in on shapes and designs of houses, landscapes and automobiles. This stayed constant throughout the drive.

The fact that Tania's mind noticed nuanced details of design patterns should not have been a surprise to either of us. Most of Tania's previous jobs have been design related: Graphic arts, manicuring, floral design, costume design, make-up artist, etc. Moreover, most of Tania's personal joys come from design-related endeavours like photography, filmmaking and landscaping. What did, however, come as something of a surprise was how much of Tania's mental attention was guided by her passions for designing. Discussing this further, Tania realised that her design passions also influenced her choices in travelling, leisure activities and friends. Her love of design guides her fondness for "backyard design" and "house flipping" television shows as well. This experiment caused us to conclude that designing is a quality of Tania's spirit—not just her ego.

Tania's insights into her spiritual identity, in turn, allowed her to better understand her job dissatisfactions. At the time Tania worked in a position that offered absolutely no creative design opportunities. Her core-self felt deprived. Meanwhile, I gained insights for coping with a source of marital dissatisfaction. I dislike cluttered environments. They can cause my mind to go into overdrive to maintain its clarity and foci. I prefer to expend my mental energies on more meaningful

117

endeavours. Tania, on the other hand, is comfortable with leaving assortments of tools, unfinished projects and creative materials throughout our house. We have argued on and off about this issue for years. By understanding Tania's spiritual quality of design, however, I could see some logic in her ways. Much of what I perceived as clutter was, to Tania, design projects in various stages of completion. Her ultimate intention has been to complete these projects and enhance our lives.

Tania started using her newfound sense of spiritual identity to improve her perspectives. She changed some of her frameworks for self-motivation. For example, Tania started framing cleaning duties as "design projects" rather than as meaningless drudgery. To help resolve our disagreements, Tania has been negotiating her methods for organising design projects with my need for clutter management. I, in turn, have found it much easier to tolerate unfinished design projects that can still appear in the house. More importantly, Tania's seeing design as a quality of her spirit has helped her grasp a core sense of her identity. Her careers may change, but Tania's spiritual gift of design will always be there.

Naturally I soon wondered what my own spiritual gifts might entail. I tried several free online "spiritual gifts inventories". Discernment kept appearing as a top spiritual gift. Discernment can actually mean different things on different levels. To St Ignatius of Loyola, "discerning spirits" meant becoming attuned to one's inner guides. Discerners detect whether they are being guided internally by Godly or ungodly forces. Discernment can also refer to a heightened ability to sense God's presence, and/or ungodly presences, in others. On more practical levels, discernment involves detecting the best solutions for solving different problems. Discernment skills allow persons to separating facts from fictions, to make important mental distinctions. Like Tania with designing, I began to see discernment at play in nearly everything I do. In my classes, I teach students how to discern social scientific truths. In my preparations, I try to discern the best methods for teaching each class. Discernment clearly guides this book. Each chapter focuses on discerning something related to spiritual journeys.

Qualities of spirit are "there" even if people do not choose to use them in Godly ways. For example, I engaged in a fair share of delinquent behaviours as a teenager. Reflecting back, I clearly see my discernment at play. I was naturally good at discerning ways of not getting caught. My spiritual gift of discernment was somewhere inside of me. I chose to use it on ungodly paths. Today when I use my discernment in Godly ways, it is accompanied by various "fruits of the spirit". Galatians (5:22) again lists these as love, joy, peace, forbearance, kindness, goodness, faithfulness, gentleness and self-control. Should I choose to use my discernment to devise ways of causing trouble and avoiding detection, I would not experience corresponding spiritual joys, love, peace, etc.

Early Christians delineated seven gifts that flow from the Holy Spirit to believers, ennobling their spiritual gifts. These are wisdom, understanding, knowledge, counsel, fortitude, piety and fear of the Lord. St Thomas Aquinas classified the first four as gifts of the mind; the last three as gifts of the will. Fortitude is the "spiritual firmness" that replaces personality rigidity in dogmatists. Fear of the Lord, or reverence, opens believers up to becoming more ennobled by God's glory. Some Christians believe that people first receive these gifts through baptism. Through confirmation, and lifelong choices to serve God, these gifts become strengthened. The gift of salvation can ennoble these gifts eternally. Applied to my own example, the Holy Spirit can ennoble my spiritual discernment with the wisdom, understanding, knowledge, counsel, piety, fortitude and reverence I'll need to fulfil my calling.

Some qualities of human spirits appear to be universal. For example, Internal Family Systems theory lists qualities believed to be inherent to the true self (or spirit). Again the "8 Cs" of IFS are calmness, curiosity, clarity, compassion, confidence, creativity, courage and connectedness. I believe chivalry is a "9th C". Recently IFS founders have added joy and harmony to their list. The seven gifts of the Holy Spirit, and the fruits of the spirit, can ennoble these inherent qualities of spirit.

Other qualities of the human spirit, however, seem more unique. Although I have met many people who share my spiritual gift of discernment, not everyone does. On the other hand, other people have spiritual gifts of hospitality and evangelisation that far exceed what I'm able to muster. Individual callings also lend uniqueness to spiritual gifts. How I use my gift of discernment, as a social scientist, differs from how a police investigator or human resources specialist would their gifts of discernment. And how I manifest my more universal spiritual qualities of creativity, courage, clarity, etc. would assuredly differ from how others do as well.

Advanced journeyers receive the additional gift of "individualised divine consciousness". A gift of God's consciousness, of His divine love, mercy, chivalry, etc., is tailored to uniquely fit each advanced journeyer. Once it is gifted it becomes something of a "master consciousness". In chapter five I mentioned that spirits, souls and egos contain their own inherent sources of consciousness. Spiritual consciousness tends to focus on freedom and transcendence. Soul consciousness is more concerned on shared meanings and connections. Individualised divine consciousness brings all of these sources of consciousness together. It also enables journeyers to "individuate" from God to some degree. God's presence stays inside of them even when they are not directly connecting with Him. Individualised divine consciousness also facilitates spiritual leadership. It gives noble agency to journeyers' spirits. This allows journeyers to reframe their experiences and truths through their own spiritual perspectives. Journeyers become even more distinct, yet more inter-connected, at the same time.

Individualised divine consciousness brings with it the added gift of "ontological security". Ontological security emerges when journeyers realise that their true qualities of spirits and soul will always be with them. Even if countless people ignore, dismiss, or fail to recognise a spiritual journeyer's chivalry, he/she will still be able to "see" it. Ontological security gives me confidence that my spiritual gift of discernment would be with me even if stranded on a deserted island. Once ontological security sets in, journeyers can travel many miles without needing other peoples' recognition or validation. Before arriving at ontological security, however, journeyers may need to experience a lot of healthy mirroring from God, the right mentors and/or loved ones.

Healthy relationships and competent mentors are central to all noble journeys. They support the soul. Mentors offer interactive self-control to those whose self-control systems may otherwise be overwhelmed. They also provide extremely important mirroring of spiritual gifts, identities and everything awakening in journeyers. Every personality part and dimension become relevant to journeyers once their mentors have seen it and reflected it back to them. This includes journeyers' emotions, thoughts, willpower, intentions, virtues, vices, gifts, strengths, wounds, etc. Mirroring helps journeyers re-assimilate their new selves, piece by mirrored piece. At some point journeyers will no longer be as dependent upon their mentors for such mirroring. But the path to independence passes through periods of healthy dependency on God and mentors.

It is worth noting that this transformative mirroring differs starkly from the kinds of social mirroring that narcissists are addicted to. As detailed, narcissists seek constant admiration for their false selves. The mirroring that narcissists solicit for their false selves, however, feeds their addictions. It never leads to satiation, liberation, holism, or awakenings. Healthier persons, on the other hand, will need a few people in their lives who can see, respect and mirror the many dimensions of their true selves. It is normal and healthy for a journeyer to want his/her truths to be validated by a few persons. It is antithetical to health to compulsively solicit mirroring for something fake, on paths leading away from growth.

Transitions from ego-based identities to spiritual ones illuminate many paradoxes. Egos serve indispensable roles. Paradoxically, pre-journey egos need a somewhat fragmented self to be able to function and navigate. However, egos are unable to resolve their own built-in contradictions (to be discussed) on their own. The inability to resolve ego contradictions prompts a person to journey. On the noble journey, spirits and souls awaken and transform. Spirits receive many gifts. Among other things, these gifts allow spirits to take over the reins of the personality. The gifts that spirits and souls bring to personalities help resolve contradictions that precipitated the ego's downfall, yet initiated the spiritual journey.

To elaborate, say a man's ego defines himself as always being strong and in control. This ego identity formed through personality splitting. Some parts of his personality needed to be exiled in order for his stronger parts to assume the helm. Any personality parts not seen as conducive to strength or control would likely be cast into his shadow. They would seemingly contradict the ego's identity as strong and in control. This man's Protector Parts would work very hard to try to keep these exiled vulnerabilities, needs, anxieties, etc. from resurfacing. For years this man's ego would do its best to navigate the overall personality. It would need some social validation for an identity as a strong person. It would also need to continue disassociating from the wounded and vulnerable parts of the personality.

Softer sides of personalities, however, allow humans to bond more deeply with others. By sacrificing intimacy to maintain a strong identity, this man would encounter many lose/lose situations. All ego identities do. In his case, the closer he moves toward intimate connections, the more likely his exiled vulnerabilities will want to resurface. On the other hand, if his ego avoids intimacy altogether, loneliness and emptiness ensue. Loneliness can deplete one's energies. Energy depletion leads to exhaustion which, in turn, creates other kinds of vulnerabilities. This ego formed its identity through separating strengths from vulnerabilities. Yet some kind of vulnerability will result from moving toward or away from intimacy. The ego would find it hard to perceive solutions.

Sooner or later false selves "fail". Despite the hard work of many Protector Parts, vulnerability will inevitably re-enter this man's personality. His ego's identity will be threatened at its very foundations. He will need to choose to journey or reinvent his false self. Egos cannot solve their inherent contradictions without spirit and soul awakenings. Once spirits and souls enter the equations, though, they perceive wins where egos see losses. The awakened spirit can invite God into both sides of the ego's divide. This man's spirit can connect with God during moments of vulnerability and invulnerability. That is a win. God will also guide him to human connections that nurture his soul. Stronger connections will fill this man up with better sources of energy, making him less vulnerable to exhaustion. That is also a win.

Ego identities are either/or. This man's ego says he is either strong or not so. Spiritual identities, however, are and/both. They transcend egos' artificial but necessary divisions. My spiritual quality of discernment is with me whether I feel strong or vulnerable, tough or soft, intuitive or rational, etc. Spiritual identities are also equipped to bring together the different parts of the personality that egos divided. My calling sometimes asks me to show certain vulnerabilities. These moments allow me to bond meaningfully, empathically and compassionately with others. On other occasions I need to be relatively invulnerable. I do not want others' pathologies to take over my classroom, my life, or others' lives. Through and/both thinking, strengths and vulnerabilities can both be parts of persons' spiritual identities. Unlike egos, spirits recognise that all parts of the personality have important roles to fulfil on God's paths. Individualised divine consciousness helps bring these truths to light.

Spiritual identities solidify through the awakened spirit's connections with God. Perhaps the deepest source of spiritual identity for Christians is that of a saved son/daughter of God. From this foundation, journeyers incorporate more of their unique and universal essential qualities as parts of their spiritual identities. Choosing to use one's spiritual gifts in God's service also allow them to be divinely ennobled. With individualised divine consciousness, a journeyer can see his/her ennobled spiritual qualities even if most people lack the capacity to. When ennobled spirits take the helm, they are equipped to guide all other personality parts toward higher nobility as well.

Transforming egos become nobler by choosing to step aside and assume advisory roles. In return they begin to heal. Transformed souls contribute energies, connections, meanings and purposes to the spirit-led self. They offer the voice of noble sacrifice for other's welfare. One's sense of calling, and individualised divine consciousness, bring the transforming spirit, soul and ego together in nobler ways. When persons' independent spirits and inter-dependent souls align, they may experience the bliss of feeling uplifted and calmed at the same time. Journeyers feel holistically noble. It is worth noting that, while soul relationships lend great purposes to callings, evolved spirits can sustain their own identities regardless of relationships. Spiritual identities include, but also transcend, friendships, marriages and careers.

For example, I believe teaching to be a significant part of my present calling. On good days, my spirit's discernment aligns with my soul's willingness to sacrifice in order to empower students to seek truths, find true meanings, live more resiliently, etc. During my best moments I feel independent and connected; uplifted and calmed. I experience a spiritual sense of "flow". This, however, is never a permanent state. More often than not, some external and/or internal event will disrupt this flow. My Protector Parts will jump back in. My ego will want to cast my softer sides into exile. Nonetheless, the fact that my spirit and soul often flow together in remarkable ways suggests that I am on the right path.

Yet my spiritual identity transcends my professorship. Egos need to attach to roles, self-images, possessions, goals, groups, relationships, etc. to form an identity. Spiritual identities, on the other hand, come from liberating connections with God. They transcend ego attachments. I certainly care about my students. My rapport with them tends to be respectful and positive. My soul finds great meaning in helping them to mature. But my spiritual identity is not tied to my occupational roles or connections. On my best days, I sacrifice for my students' journeys out of my higher relationship with God. My connections with God guide me to offer students the kindness, firmness, humour, compassion, encouragement, etc. they need. My spirit, however, remains unattached to classroom outcomes. If students do not work to their potential, it does not phase my spiritual identity. It irritates me. My soul wants better things for them, but my spiritual identity transcends these outcomes. These same issues used to drive my ego nuts. My ego's identity was linked to the outcome of students working to their potential. It was set up for frustration.

Egos and spirits identify with chivalry in much different ways. Egos develop chivalrous identities by attaching themselves to roles, duties and self-images they see as noble. For pre-journey selves that is desirable. It is immensely better for egos to try to be chivalrous than to not try to. The realm of the ego has limitations, however. To the aforementioned ego, chivalry would be tied to being strong and in control. A man's exiled vulnerabilities would equal non-chivalry to him. In contrast, spiritual identities see how chivalry connects with potentially any part of the personality. The spirit sees that sometimes it can be chivalrous to drop one's guard and offer compassionate soul connection to others. At other times it serves chivalry to be tough and guarded. The ego's sense of chivalry is, by necessity, divided. Spiritual chivalry is holistic and inclusive.

The ultimate source of all chivalry is God, its inventor. When the awakened chivalry of human spirits moves toward God's holy chivalry, potentials for human chivalry skyrocket. All callings are spiritually chivalrous, albeit in different ways. Each spiritual gift helps journeyers to chivalrously meet the challenge of their calling, one step at a time. Individualised divine consciousness, ontological security and spiritual identity helps journeyers persevere and transform on paths of higher chivalry, even when other people do not respect or understand their journey. The inherent chivalry of human spirits becomes ennobled by the gifts of the Holy Spirit. All gifts bestowed upon human spirits equip them to lead the overall personality toward God. Egos increase chivalry by stepping aside. Souls become more chivalrous in their sacrifices for higher causes. In advanced journeyers, a unique nobility of spirit coalesces from many different sources of chivalry.

Spirit-led selves bring chivalry into two separate worlds. In earthly worlds, journeyers devote more time and energy to the causes of their callings. These actions ennoble the overall personality—and are very necessary. The global society of today contains no shortage of oppression, poverty, exploitation, human slavery, terrorism, war, etc. Journeyers are called upon to chivalrously offer spiritual strength, gifts and leadership to the resolution of such issues. In the spiritual world, spirits continue to grow through connections with God's divine chivalry. To my beliefs, the challenges of spiritual leadership and chivalry continue well into the afterlife; and so do the benefits.

(13)

Transforming the Shadow

At one point or another, every piece of a journeyer's personality will make itself known. This includes Exiles and wounds, the topics of the next two chapters. During intensive transformation periods, the internal worlds of journeyers become very busy places. Numerous personality fragments rise from deeper soul regions. For spirits to effectively lead the overall person, they must develop respectful relationships with a host of different personality parts. Some personality parts will simply need validation and acceptance. Others will need to be healed, cleansed and/or transformed.

If not reconciled, surfacing vices, archetypes, wounds and even positive traits can sidetrack a journey. Each personality part carries its own intentions. Some parts' intentions, when untransformed, are antithetical to journeying. On the other hand, effective internal work facilitates spiritual chivalry and vice versa. Journeyers who transform their personality parts have more substance, strength and resources to chivalrously offer to their surrounding worlds. They will also be less held back by internal conflict. It should be noted that wound and Exile work cycles. Brief but constructive periods of inner turmoil are typically followed by times of inner peace, contentment and harmony. And all such moments can serve the journey, journeyer and God.

Many pre-journey selves are trapped, some without realising it. Ego traps can be normalised in groups and cultures. The ego's shackles come from a variety of external and internal sources. External situations become traps when egos perceive lose/lose situations. Interpersonal relationships, bureaucracies, structures, families, workplaces and larger culture can all put egos in situations where they, say, perceive losses if they assert themselves and if they do not. Addictions, wounds, trauma, sin and fear are among potential internal shackles. It is worth noting that spiritually awakened journeyers are not necessarily fully liberated, healed, or pure. Temptations to revisit sins still return. Spiritual journeyers can continue to carry places of brokenness, darkness and incompletion within them for many miles. Even on noble journeys, most wounds never attain one-hundred-percent healing. Journeyers achieve "good enough" healing and "good enough" transformation to serve God with spiritual chivalry and fulfil their callings.

The term 'shadow' does not necessarily refer to human darkness, though it can. To Carl Jung, the shadow entailed anything that has been exiled or hidden from the conscious self. Castaway aspects of personalities can include positive and negative qualities. Authenticity, for instance, may be exiled into the shadows of persons raised in narcissistic families. When authentic qualities of people are consistently degraded, dismissed, or shamed, they may go underground to survive. Similarly, human dignity can live in the shadows of those whose social worlds have demeaned it. This can also be true for chivalry.

Yet, as mentioned, exiled personality parts do not stay underground forever. They can resurface in the slip of the tongue, impulses, dreams, addictions, compulsions, illnesses, emotional outbursts, etc. Sometimes their surfacing leads to public dismay. The national news routinely reports on public figures that appeared to be principled and/or chivalrous, then shock the public by engaging in deviant sexual behaviour. A Jungian interpretation would suggest that buried pieces of these celebrities' personalities found ways to express themselves. Hiding one's darker impulses behind public personas does not make them go away. All Exiles long to express themselves. When ignored for too long, some may express themselves in aberrant ways.

Internal Family Systems (IFS) theory, discussed in chapter five, provides numerous tools, resources and mental maps for transforming one's Exiles, Protectors and true selves (spirits). As mentioned, Exiles are personality parts that have been driven into the shadows. Carrying intense pain, fear, shame, trauma, etc., they threaten to overwhelm a person's control systems if they resurface. Manager (Protector) Parts try to keep Exiles from resurfacing. A critical voice, for example, may try to keep Exiles in the shadows by berating them. Yet Exiles find ways of rising to consciousness anyway. They want and need to be heard. When this occurs, Firefighter (Protector) Parts enter in to manage the situation. Exiles and Protector Parts are linked together. One cannot heal his/her Exiles without first encountering parts assigned to protect them.

Alcoholism was offered as an example of Protector Parts. Many alcoholics use intoxicants to "self-medicate" their underlying wounds and traumas (Exiles). An addict will likely carry large numbers of Protectors. Denial, for example, can be a strong Protector Part. Lying, grandiosity and manipulative behaviour may be as well. When alcoholics experience guilt or shame over their intoxicated behaviours, their "Firefighter" Protectors may step in for damage control. A Firefighter Part may try to disarm other people with apologies. Over time, an alcoholic's protective system can become very complex. These systems, however, are doing what they are designed to do. They are protecting persons from being overwhelmed by buried emotions, wounds and traumas. It is easy for alcoholics to become victims of their Protector Parts' successes. The same parts that keep Exiles at bay can prevent people from journeying.

IFS treatment might start by helping an alcoholic client become mindful of his/her various Protector Parts. How IFS advices people to relate to their Protectors, though, may seem to go against common sense. Clients are instructed to not judge, shame, or berate their own Protector Parts (even if these parts engage in unhealthy behaviours). Judgment and shaming only magnify the intensity and intention of Protectors. Internal conflicts amplify. Clients are instead advised to talk to their Protector Parts respectfully, from places of compassion and curiosity. When Protectors are treated with compassion and respect, they tend to relax. All personality parts want to be heard. If treated respectfully, an alcoholic Protector Part will likely be very willing to discuss where it came from, and exactly how it has helped to protect the person.

As time progresses, clients establish respectful relations with more and more of their parts. They offer validation and compassion to each one. A client may even thank his/her own alcoholic Protector Parts for their years of protecting him/her. This, again, may seem counter-intuitive to some. There is, however, much logic to it. Once Protectors feel appreciated, they relax. As mentioned, all exiled parts are linked to Protector Parts. When Protectors relax, Exiles have opportunities to rise up and heal. Exiles too have stories to tell. Often, they have been carrying intense burdens of sorrow, disappointment, fear, etc. From places of curiosity and compassion, clients begin to listen to their own Exiles' stories; to experience their emotional intensities. As clients offer validation and compassion to their Exiles, their emotional intensities lessen. Eventually Exiles can be unburdened from pain they have carried. Their liberation allows them to contribute renewed energy and resources to the overall self.

As Exiles heal, Protectors have less to protect. Their workloads are lightened. In many cases, they will need new assignments and purpose. An alcoholic Protector Part would no longer need to take the wheel, and steer a person toward a liquor store, if the underlying Exiles have been relatively healed and reintegrated. By the time such changes occur, clients will have formed more trusting relationships with many of their personality parts. Out of these relationships, clients can ask their own Protectors what new roles they would like to play. Protector Parts are likely to offer suggestions. Odds are an alcoholic Protector was never too interested in problematic drinking to begin with. Instead, it could distract the overwhelmed mind through more constructive practises. Exercising and journaling are among examples. It could also jump in and speak empowering quotes or mantras to the distressed mind. After healing work, Protector Parts can change roles in ways that better facilitate chivalry for the overall personality.

As clients work to heal their Exiles and transform their Protector Parts, their "true selves" (or spirit) become more involved. In IFS theory, Protectors and Exiles are seen as important parts of the true self. The self, however, is much more than the sum total of its assembly of Protectors and Exiles. It is of a deeper essence. Again, IFS argues that true selves contain inherent calmness, curiosity, clarity, compassion, confidence, creativity, courage, connectedness, joy and harmony. I would add chivalry. Working on one's parts facilitates chivalry in several ways. When Protector Parts transform and true selves take the helm, inherent chivalry becomes active in the overall personality. Healing one's Exiles is also facilitative of chivalry. Journeyers have more energy, and inner integrity, to take chivalrous actions in the world. Protectors, in turn, can make conscious choices to assume roles more conducive to chivalry.

The same rules would apply to narcissism and dogmatism. As suggested, contempt for outsiders, rigidity and scapegoating behaviours are among dogmatists' Protector Parts. Their deeper Exiles include emotional turmoil, insecurity and intense fears. The primary Protector Part for narcissists is the persona. False selves protect narcissists from deeper Exiles that may, with life and death intensity, overwhelm minds with fears of failure and worthlessness. When a narcissist's Exiles begin to surface, his/her self-image steps in to protect the mind from short-circuiting. As mentioned, narcissists' and dogmatists' protector can be so adept at their roles, however, that they can impede spiritual growth for years. Persons' Exiles do not heal. Their true selves do not awaken. Protectors do not transform into roles more conducive to spiritual chivalry.

A spiritual journey, however, creates opportunities for any kind of Protector Part to transform. For example, a narcissist's grandiosity protects him/her from deeper feelings of worthlessness. Who could feel worthless when one's Protector Part says he/she is of epic greatness? Grandiosity also energises. It lifts narcissists up. On a spiritual journey a grandiose Protector Part could let go of its belief that it is unequivocally great and/or better than other people. It could replace this with a healthier striving for excellence on a path toward God. A transformed Protector would be more compatible with spiritual chivalry in providing authentic lifts related to God's divine chivalry. Deeper feelings of worthlessness, once protected by grandiosity, could then begin to surface and heal.

For many people, smartphones are functional tools. For numerous iGeners, however, smartphones are intertwined with dominant Protector Parts. When they begin to sense the surfacing of exiled insecurities, smartphone-addicted Protector Parts jump in. Smartphones distract the mind from underlying fears, while giving users some form of validation for their individuality. Smartphones also offer connections that are emotionally safe. They sidestep risks of face-to-face communication. Unfortunately, these smartphone Protector Parts are so good at what they do that many young adults are not learning resilience, or moving toward spirit/soul awakenings. Again, one cannot develop spiritual chivalry without taking reasonable emotional, social and physical risks. It will be interesting to see how journeying iGens will transform these Protector Parts.

Internal Family Systems theory was designed to fit a wide gamut of secular and religious models of growth. Yet the best outcomes, in my opinion, occur when healthy religious traditions and IFS work together. Humans can awaken their true selves or spirits without a belief in God. Faith, however, allows the fruits of the spirit and gifts of the Holy Spirit to ennoble and guide the awakening spirit. The master consciousness that links spirit, soul and ego consciousnesses together comes only from God. A sense of calling is needed for spirits and souls to integrate. Many other spiritual gifts and resources are invaluable in helping journeyers comprehend and reconcile their shadows and wounds.

Sin is another issue that makes religious practises advantageous for growth. Some Protector Parts are intertwined with certain sins. Idolatry can release dopamine in a person's brain, giving a "lift" from depression. The sin is "protective" in this sense, though it blocks one's connection with God. When Protector Parts are shackled to sin, they may need more than just compassion, validation and opportunities to share their stories. Sinful Protector Parts also benefit from religious reconciliation, such as "confession" in the Catholic faith, and/or prayer, to restore a relationship with God. For example, revenge can protect people from experiencing exiled feelings of powerlessness and victimisation. When one walks away from divine justice, in attempts to vindicate his/her ego's beliefs, the journey sidetracks. Through religious interventions, though, healthy desires for justice can be liberated from the oppression of revenge.

An "and/both" view suggests that a journeyer can seek religious reconciliation for his/her sins *and* dialogue compassionately with his/her sinful Protector Parts. On a spiritual journey, a transforming vengeful Protector Part could be asked if it is willing to keep its desires for justice, yet defer the ultimate outcomes to God. If a vengeful Protector agrees and relaxes, deeper feelings of powerlessness and victimisation begin to heal. The formerly vengeful Protector Part can find a new role. Perhaps it can agree to be a servant of God's divine justice. From places of compassion and curiosity, journeyers negotiate such changes with many of their personality parts. Respectful internal relationships make it possible for Protector Parts to agree to new roles and transform. Faith, in turn, allows God to enter into any area of the human shadow. The Holy Spirit can bring divine gifts to potentially all Protector Parts. Connections with divine love encourage all personality parts to choose nobler roles.

Shadow work creates opportunities for new strengths, virtues, resiliencies and coping skills to develop. Mindfulness is one such resource. Among other things, mindfulness allows people to experience intense emotions and temptations without becoming controlled by them. Say, for example, that a person with a vengeful Protector Part engages in mindfulness. His/her first step would be to recognise the vengeful part from a place of mentally detached curiosity. With mindfulness, one simply observes his/her thoughts, desires and emotions without reaction or judgment. This allows people to be present with their parts without fuelling sin or negativity. It also opens doors for respectful interaction.

A mindful person may ask a part, 'What is the truth that you wish to express?' A Personality Part can then do what it longs to do, express its truth. In the case of a vengeful part, its underlying desire for justice can be validated. Transformational processes can begin. Eventually the journeyer can more effectively, and chivalrously, take up causes of justice in ways that enhance his/her loves, virtues, gifts, etc. The journeyer's spirit, not his/her revenge, will be placed at the helm. Mindfulness allows one to be present with, and counsel, virtually all Personality Parts in their various stages of healing and transformation. This counsel, in turn, can be guided by the Holy Spirit's divine counsel.

In Carl Jung's view, the human shadow can also be a place of hidden "archetypes". Archetypes are blueprints for personalities or "sub-personalities" that carry distinctive energies with them. Jung believed that some archetypes are universal to all people across cultures. For example, he believed all men carry archetypes for a feminine "sub-personality" called the anima. Similarly, every woman possesses an animus or masculine side. Carl Jung also believed that archetypes emerged from a collective unconscious, shared by everyone. Archetypes may be part of the DNA of human souls. To Carl Jung, mentally healthy persons are those mature in their archetypes. They integrate archetypal energies and intentions into an individuating self. Neurosis, on the other hand, is related to persons being split off from their deeper sources of energy. In these cases, archetypes may hide in the shadow, remain immature and foster destructive behaviours.

Jungian scholars have identified a long list of potential archetypes. This chapter will discuss four of them. Moore and Gillette wrote extensively on the "King/Queen", "warrior", "magician" and "lover" archetypes. The authors propose that every person in every culture possesses all four. When mature, the King/Queen, Warrior, Magician and/or Lover archetypes contribute different energies, intentions and resources to the spirit-led self and surrounding world. Every mature archetype, in its own way, helps spiritual journeyers to fulfil their callings. Each is facilitative of a different kind of chivalry. On the other hand, immature shadow forms of these archetypes can exert destructive pulls over overall personalities.

Moore and Gillette describe the basic structures of these archetypes as triangle shaped. At the apexes of the triangular structures, more mature versions of the King/Queen, Warrior, Magician and Lover can reside. Healthy archetypes energise and empower people's true selves. On the other hand, the bases of these triangles contain two opposing and immature "shadows" of each archetype (at each end). One shadow pole propels one into some kind of action. The other shadow pole lends energy to inaction. Every shadow pole also carries its own intentions. In raw form, archetypal shadows are distinctive energy sources. As shadows solidify, they can become their own Protector Parts and/or Exiles.

According to Moore and Gillette, a mature Lover archetype contributes much compassion, mercy, joy, humanity and meaning to life. Persons mature in their Lover archetypes are more concerned with giving unselfish love than receiving it. They channel mature energy of love toward causes higher than themselves. Agape love is an inherently chivalrous love. Journeyers chivalrous in love live with more joy and purpose. For journeyers' Lover archetypes to evolve, however, the two shadow poles will need to be addressed. The authors refer to the active shadow of the Lover archetype (existing at one side of the base of the triangle) as the "Addict". In its raw forms, the Addict shadow is preoccupied with pleasure-seeking. It sees hedonism as an end unto itself. In immature persons, Addict parts can seize control of the whole personality for periods of time. Persons controlled by their Addict shadow may succumb to a host of addictions including drugs, gambling, work, sex, pornography, social media, food, etc.

The authors refer to the opposite shadow of the Lover archetype as the "Impotent Lover". Its energies induce passivity and dreamy states of inactivity. Persons controlled by the Impotent Lover part may prefer fantasy lives to real challenges that accompany truly intimate relationships. The impotent lover shadow tends to negate zest and life force, contributing to depression. It is worth noting that the opposing energies of each archetypal shadow can counteract one another; albeit in ways hindering growth. When people find themselves consumed by their addict shadow's hedonism, they can shut down their passions by activating the opposite shadow pole of their Lover archetype. They can gain some sense of control over their hedonistic drive. However, when split off from their Addict energies, emotional lifelessness can result. Depression may take over. To then counteract depression, they may reengage their addict shadows. Immature pursuits of pleasure become re-ignited. Addictions may again resume control.

Some persons spend their whole lives going back and forth from one archetypal shadow pole to its opposite, without ever travelling upwards. Idolatry can be a temptation for immature archetypal shadows; thus, a snare for overall personalities.

Most addictions involve idolatry in some form. Gambling addicts can make idols out of money. Exercise addicts make idols out of their own bodies. The impotent lover shadow, in turn, may make idols out of recurring fantasies and images of lost lovers. When journeyers' hearts choose paths of spiritual chivalry over idolatry, however, archetypes begin to mature. Growth in the Lover archetype accompanies choices to offer love unselfishly and chivalrously.

As Addict and Impotent Lover parts transform, they contribute better energies to the overall personality without taking it over. These changes can be facilitated through dialoguing with one's archetypal shadow parts, as mapped by Internal Family Systems theory. In a new role, a transforming Addict can encourage persons to constructively enjoy some of life's pleasures. To enjoy dinner, drinks and conversation after a long workweek seems compatible with most persons' journeys. The transforming addict part could essentially provide the voice of modest pleasure pursuit, without taking over the person. Similarly, a transforming impotent lover part can encourage journeyers to reflect sentimentally, and/or drift away into healthier fantasies. These moments, too, can serve the noble journey.

The ability to draw energy from one's archetypal shadows, without becoming consumed by them, increases greatly in spirit-led selves. Gifts of individualised divine consciousness, mindfulness, self-control, etc. become extremely important assets to these processes. According to Moore and Gillette, any shadow of any archetype can potentially exert a magnetic downward pull on one's conscious mind. Diligent parts work may be required for one to learn to access his/her shadow energies, from plateaus of maturity, without succumbing to their downward pull. This is especially true in one's areas of greatest difficulties. I have never known someone fully mature in all four of these archetypes. Most journeyers I know struggle daily with the downward pull of at least one archetypal shadow. It is part of their spiritual journeys to do so. Many non-journeyers, however, seem to struggle with the downward pulls of many of their archetypal shadows.

Maturing in one's Lover archetype, growing in agape, is central to everyone's calling. No noble journey sidesteps awakenings of higher love en route to God's divine love. On many occasions, though, journeyers will need to spring into action, persevere through adversity and protect themselves, their loved ones and their principles. Indeed, these actions are compatible with chivalrous love, but they are often energised by a different archetype. The mature Warrior archetype energises people to act quickly and decisively, think rapidly and clearly, persevere and use aggressive energy toward a constructive end. Persons mature in their Warrior archetypes live by codes of honour. They chivalrously fight for causes higher and larger than those of their egos, often defending the vulnerable and downtrodden. They are also fully capable of mercy. Paths to Warrior archetype maturity, however, are certainly not easy.

The Warrior archetype also carries two shadow forms, which Moore and Gillette call the "Sadist" and the "Masochist". People controlled by their sadist shadow may use their aggressive energy to oppress or scapegoat others. For example, most narcissists and dogmatists have not mastered these Warrior shadows. Domestic violence, terrorism and bullying can be linked to the control of the Sadist. On the other hand, persons controlled by their masochistic shadow find pleasure in absorbing abuses. As suggested in chapter eight, Masochists may tacitly agree to being oppressed in order to feel a sense of their own control. Like persons immature in their lover archetypes, less mature warriors can "swing" back and forth between their two shadows. Most bullies turn into masochists when effectively confronted. Conversely, some Masochists become Sadists when opportunities to oppress vulnerable persons present themselves.

Mature Warriors learn to access energies from both shadow poles without being controlled by either. For example, the energies of a transforming Sadist part can help journeyers to strike down lies, think quickly, declare and defend boundaries, subdue predatory persons, etc. Similarly, transforming masochistic parts can lend a pain resistance that is often needed for absorbing life's blows and moving ahead. When athletic coaches yell to exhausted players 'Gotta love it', they are calling forth positive uses for masochistic energies.

Historically, hunter and gatherer tribes guided all young males into Warrior maturity. During manhood rites, Warrior energies were ritually awakened in the company of mature elders. Elders taught neophytes how to harness and constructively channel their powerful aggressive energies. Young warriors acquired respect, honour and self-control for their aggressive energies. They lived by their tribes' versions of chivalry. Unfortunately, in the US today, mature elders seem in short supply. Yet the needs for many young males to see and define themselves as warriors remain strong. Boys not escorted into manhood by true warriors may seek substitutes. Many young males engage in pseudo manhood rites offered by street gangs, survivalist groups, terrorist cells, etc. In addition, US prisons are full of people controlled by the shadows of their Warrior archetypes.

A general fear of human aggression sometimes wafts in the air in American culture today. Such fears can be valid. Many who are controlled by their sadistic shadows have done horrific things. Moore and Gillette's view, however, suggests that the root of the problem relates more to archetypal immaturity than to human aggression itself. Aggression can have many constructive uses. Spiritual journeyers are not people who never feel aggressive. They are people mature in their uses of aggression. Moore and Gillette's view casts a somewhat different spin on issues of bullying. Because all persons in all cultures possess the Warrior archetype (and Sadist shadow), any boy or girl, in any culture or neighbourhood, could bully.

Abusive, toxic, or violent social environments can ratchet up persons' sadistic tendencies. But if anti-bullying policies only serve to drive sadistic impulses underground, they never address the root problem. Some adolescents repress their sadistic energies during school hours, and then release them in the evenings through cyber-bullying. These youth are not being taught to mature as warriors. Better anti-bullying solutions would involve teaching boys and girls how to respect, harness, mature and utilise their Warrior energies. Their spiritual journeys may someday ask them to be warriors for Godly causes.

American culture seems to make two large mistakes in its treatment of the Warrior archetype. One is to deny that aggressive energies can be inherent and/or constructive to humankind. Indiscriminately demonising human aggression can drive it underground to places where it does not mature. The other error involves supersizing the Warrior archetype. The culture sometimes elevates this archetype to places of importance above and beyond the other archetypes. Neither currently provides the healthy Warrior archetype with a proper place in the spirit-led self. Indeed, the Warrior archetype is extremely important. In periods of combat, conflict and/or immediate crisis, the Warrior can be the most important archetype. Yet in countless other kinds of situations, the Lover, King/Queen and Magician may be the more contributory archetype. Each mature archetype contributes different chivalrous energies to the spirit-led self, helping journeyers to fulfil their callings.

The healthy King or Queen archetype contributes rules, structure and organisation to the human personality and/or surrounding worlds. Moore and Gillette propose that the King/Queen archetype often develops last. When it does mature, often in midlife, it lends governance to the energies and intentions of the other archetypes. Among other things, mature Kings/Queens provide healthy limits that true freedom, self-control and effective group functioning depend upon. Healthy Kings/Queens know how to create order out of chaos. They chivalrously empower others rather than oppressing them. Mature Kings/Queens also walk with their own authority. They possess inner authority whether their social worlds anoint them with formal outer authority or not. Jesus Christ, Gandhi and Nelson Mandela are examples of persons very evolved in the King archetype.

Less mature people, however, may be controlled by the shadows of this archetype. Moore and Gillette refer to the active King/Queen shadow as the "Tyrant". Persons possessed by their Tyrant shadow seek power for power sake. Today's world has no shortage of people consumed by their Tyrant. Tyrants, in turn, need dogmatic followers and/or scapegoats to oppress. On the other hand, the inactive King/Queen shadow is termed the "Weakling". Persons controlled by their Weakling shadows give up their own power too readily. Many father figures on television sitcoms are portrayed as buffoons. Being unable to wield ordinary fatherly authority, they represent the pull of the Weakling shadow. Spiritual journeyers, however, draw energies from both King/Queen shadows without being controlled by them. Transforming Tyrant parts can allow journeyers to take charge of situations warranting leadership and/or governance. A journeyer could also heed advice from his/her transforming Weakling part to not waste energies in areas he/she cannot control. The path of King/Queen maturation involves persons claiming their own power, yet using it chivalrously in the service of others.

Finally, the mature Magician archetype energises the human mind to master knowledge. Magicians' knowledge domains could be religious and/or scientific, vocational and/or academic, intuitive and/or logical, etc. The information age seems to have put the Magician archetype in overdrive. People who spend hours each day online are more consistently connected to their Magician energies than were their predecessors. When healthy, the Magician archetype assists persons in detaching from their emotions. Mindfulness is also linked to the Magician. In crises, the mature archetype helps one's mind rise above distressed emotions and maintains clear thinking. Moore and Gillette also link the "mind's eye" to the magician archetype. When mature, the Magician archetype enables journeyers to assimilate and utilise countless sources of knowledge toward constructive, ethical and chivalrous ends.

The active shadow pole of the Magician archetype is termed the "Manipulator". In the throes of the Manipulator, people use their knowledge and skills to deceive and exploit others for self-serving purposes. Today's narcissism epidemic suggests that many are controlled by overactive Manipulator shadows. On the other hand, the inactive shadow is called the "Innocent One". Persons controlled by this shadow may hide nastier intentions behind veils of innocence. All too often, when manipulative persons are called to the carpet, they swing to the Innocent One shadow and play dumb. Healthy development for the Magician archetype involves choosing to use one's knowledge, energies and skills in mature and principled ways. With persons' compasses are set toward God, the Magician archetype can facilitate countless chivalrous uses of knowledge.

It is worth noting that transformations in one archetype can trigger growth in others. When Lover archetypes evolve into agape love, a person's Warrior parts find higher causes to fight for, Kings/Queens gains better directions for their powers, and Magicians receive higher purposes for their knowledge. On the other hand, transgressions in one archetype can trigger downward spirals in others. To be sure, awakenings of archetypal shadows present some dangers, along with countless opportunities. Due to the dangers, it is unwise for non-advanced journeyers to attempt archetypal self-therapy without the assistance of competent mentors and God. Spirits gifted with individualised divine consciousness can handle their minds being flooded with raw archetypal energies. Many egos cannot.

The noble journey guides people to the right mentors for each archetype, on God's timeline. A number of parents, grandparents and bosses have evolved in their King/Queen archetypes. Many relationship counsellors, religious leaders and happily married elders can serve as mentors for the Lover archetype. Seasoned coaches, soldiers and martial arts instructors are among a given community's mentors for the Warrior archetype. Teachers, professionals and religious leaders are among mentors for the Magician. Should a person choose to step into a journey, it is likely that the right mentors will appear for the right archetypes at the right time.

As mentioned, energies and intentions of archetypal shadows can become intertwined with various personality parts. The Sadist and Tyrant shadows energise a number of control-oriented Protector Parts. Narcissistic personas can draw energies from the Manipulator shadow of the magician. Yet the methods for dialoguing with one's archetypal shadows stay the same. From places of curiosity and compassion, journeyers can call upon their archetypal parts to share their stories. Like other personality parts, archetypal shadows long for validation. They transform through their willingness to assume healthier roles. For example, a transforming Sadist can agree to help strike down lies and/or protect others from bullying without becoming a bully. With compasses set toward God, all of a journeyer's shadow parts can transform into positive forces.

To reiterate, mature Magician archetypes help journeyers attain and apply the many diverse sources of knowledge that their paths will require. The healthy Warrior helps people act quickly and decisively, think clearly, persevere despite obstacles and protect themselves, their loved ones and their beliefs. Meanwhile, mature King/Queen archetypes lend structure, inner authority and organisation to journeys and journeyers. The evolved Lover opens up the human heart. It provides compassion, purpose, meaning and connectedness. When the inherent chivalry of awakened spirits connects with mature archetypes, journeyers become more chivalrous in their offerings of inner power, aggressive, knowledge and love.

Shadow work may begin with "dark nights of the soul" yet can last a lifetime. Again, the shadow houses a host of positive and negative qualities that, for one reason or another, have split off from ego identities. Sooner or later spiritual journeys will awaken all shadow parts. One step at a time, on God's timelines, spirit-led journeyers claim these once-hidden parts of their personalities. First steps might involve dialoguing with a given personality part from a place of mindfulness, compassion and curiosity. Buried positive parts may need to be assured that it is safe to re-join the personality. Protector Parts may seek validation for roles they have played (even if they created dysfunction in the process). Sinful Protector Parts may also need religious reconciliation in order for their underlying intentions to be truly liberated; and for connections with divine sources of chivalry to be restored.

(14)

Transcending Traumas

Nearly every human being is wounded in some respects. As mentioned, wounds serve many important functions for the noble spiritual journey. Often it is a person's wounds that motivate them to journey, to step into the unknown to begin with. Wounds can also prompt false selves and rigid worldviews to crumble, paving the way for true selves to emerge. They carve a space in the personality for future gifts to reside in. In addition, wounds help open channels with God. Meanwhile, journeyers' efforts to heal their wounds can facilitate noble soul relationships and spiritual self-mastery.

The last chapter discussed how Internal Family Systems theory can help journeyers transform their Protector Parts and heal their Exiles. The same methods are facilitative of trauma recovery. For example, IFS theory asserts that healing is made possible by treating their Personality Parts with respect and compassion. A recent study by Dahm et al. found that war veterans high in self-compassion were less likely to develop PTSD than those lower in it. On the other hand, trauma can be accompanied by very complex sets of Protector Parts and Exiles. Survivors may need to renegotiate their survival responses to traumatic stimuli. Additional tools and resources need to supplement IFS approaches to recovery. This chapter focuses on such nuances of trauma recovery. As with shadow work, recovery is best facilitated when the spirit-led self receives guidance from the Holy Spirit.

Anyone in any culture could develop PTSD, though some groups are at higher risk. In addition to war veterans, victims of domestic violence, bullying and sex trafficking have increased risks for developing PTSD. The cruelties that can surround these persons may diminish their ability to give themselves compassion. Self-medication is a common Protector Part for persons with PTSD. A significant percentage of people in drug/alcohol treatment centres and 12-step groups meet PTSD criteria. Staying on the move serves self-protective purposes. It keeps Exiles at bay. A high percentage of runaways and homeless adults meet criteria for PTSD as well.

The twenty first century has already witnessed advancements in the knowledge and treatment of Post-Traumatic Stress Disorder. Newer counselling techniques help people relatively recover at faster rates than before. And an "and/both" perspective allows trauma recovery to be a scientific and religious journey at the same time. Journeyers can use scientific technology to relatively recover on paths leading toward spiritual chivalry and God. The scientific advances of Peter Levine and Robert Scaer will now be discussed. Both authors illuminate important connections between PTSD, social circumstances and the fight, flight and freeze instincts of the survival brain. Their combined works offer compelling models for not just individual trauma recovery, but larger scale societal reform.

Peter Levine spent years observing survival strategies in animals. In particular, Levine focused on animals' instincts for fighting, fleeing and freezing. He noted that traumatic reactions are, to a large degree, instinctive. They are connected with animals' default instincts for "freezing" in certain situations. When animals perceive life-threatening situations, to which they believe they cannot fight or flee, freeze responses are instinctively activated. The freeze response is exemplified by a deer in the headlights. Freeze responses signal the body to prepare for certain death. The brain is altered. People and animals experience "out of body" states of consciousness. In Levine's view, the freeze response is nature's built-in mercy system. It prevents the organism from experiencing the most intense pains of death. Frozen by headlights, deer feel less of the impact of automobiles.

Sometimes, however, people and animals survive experiences that triggered the freeze response. How they respond to the survival will greatly influence whether they develop resilience or PTSD symptoms. Levine believes all animals possess "trauma recovery" instincts. Once danger

143

subsided, wild animals instinctively activate "freeze discharge" systems. To discharge freeze-related energies, their bodies shake involuntarily for brief periods of time. These processes are, again, guided by recovery instincts. If not discharged, freeze-related energy becomes stored in the body. In the human world, stored-up freeze energies contribute to numerous physical and/or mental illnesses, including depression, high blood pressure, insomnia, dissociation, stomach issues, headaches, etc.

Discharging freeze allows wild animals to avoid PTSD. They instinctively let their bodies shake it off. Many human beings, however, are not in touch with these instincts. Humans may suppress (or exile) freeze energies instead of releasing them. Some perhaps fear the momentary losses of control associated with the discharge. Others may wish to avoid emotionally intense states that can accompany discharge processes. In the human world, many external and internal forces can hinder basic instincts for releasing freeze-related energies. These energies instead become stored up in persons' minds and bodies. The clusters of physical and mental symptoms that correlate can be referred to as PTSD.

People can "visit" freeze without "living there". Freezing does not automatically translate into PTSD. An unexpected loud explosion next door could trigger an instinctive freeze response. The initial freeze response heightens awareness, allowing one to evaluate potential threats. Once a person diagnoses the noise's source, he/she may choose to fight, flee, or not worry about it. Choosing any of these options will enable people to shift out of freeze-related states. These moments of "functional freezing", however, can translate into PTSD when they become conditioned responses and freeze energies are not discharged.

For example, children abused by their fathers may become conditioned to freezing when in their fathers' presence. They may not know when the next attack will occur. Freezing proactively around their fathers can be a default survival strategy. Small children are not able to fight or flee larger abusers. If these children also perceive their abuses as life-threatening, their survival brains would instinctively activate freeze. Children protecting themselves by freezing around their fathers, however, may begin do so around others reminding them of their fathers. Over time the freeze instinct can become linked to a dominant Protector Part. It can take-over whenever one is in the vicinity of potentially abusive people. Simultaneously, stored-up freeze energies would be a host of physical and mental health difficulties.

It is worth emphasising that not every adverse situation is conducive to PTSD. Bureaucracies can create numerous aggravating situations that are not easily fought or fled. When these situations are not life or ego-identity threatening, though, they are considered "pains in the neck". Similarly, situations that pose threats yet can be effectively fought or fled do not translate into PTSD. Again, the freeze response is instinctively activated when persons/animals are in situations that: (1) They believe they cannot fight or flee; and (2) They perceive to be life-threatening. In human worlds, threats to the ego identity can elicit the same responses as threats to life. To persons who have not yet journeyed, the thought of losing their ego identity can be as fear-provoking as that of physical death. Their spirits are not prepared to take over and lead them.

When threats to the ego identity combine with threats of physical harm, the potential for PTSD magnifies. For example, say that a father and husband named John is consistently bullied at work by his boss. Say this boss is controlled by his Sadist and Tyrant shadow parts. John's family needs his income to survive. His ego identity is attached to his job and role as a provider. Fleeing the situation may not seem to be a viable option. John would risk losing his income and identity. John could also lose his job and ego identity if he fought his sadistic boss. Unable to fight or flee a threatening situation, John would be susceptible to PTSD. His survival brain may begin to activate the freeze response around his boss. Over time, freeze consciousness can engulf more and more aspects of John's personality and life. His mind and body slow down as a result. John's stored-up freeze energies may contribute to anxiety, depression and physical illness. His concentration and productivity decrease. This, in turn, gives a sadistic boss more reasons to pounce on him. Unfortunately, situations like this are fairly common in American workplaces.

Internal Family Systems theory can shed light on what may happen next. PTSD causes many personality parts to go into exile. The parts of John that experience joy, spontaneity, hope and even fight/flight energies, might be stuffed away. Many aspects of John's true self would disappear as well. PTSD does not, however, shut down all personality parts. Protector Parts become overactive. John may don a mask of the non-confrontational employee who is happy to obey to his boss. As John's energies become depleted, addiction-related Protector Parts may offer him some options. These Protectors may, for example, drive John to excessive use of alcohol, food, sex, etc. in an attempt to energise his survival. Surviving, however, is not the same thing as thriving. To survive, John will likely split himself off from parts of his personality that experience harmony, contentment, joy, spontaneity, etc.

Recovery is more possible today than ever before. Levine's research illuminated a pivotal recovery process called "re-negotiation". During traumatic experiences, freeze responses are chosen instinctively by the survival brain. Over time the brains of persons with PTSD can become wired to freeze-related Protector Parts. Re-negotiation involves changing this wiring. One step at a time, persons in recovery reactivate the intense mind-sets that initially selected freeze, in order to select a different option. To do so, they may need to first put themselves in situations that remind their survival brains of those that first triggered freezing. God, of course, can be invited into this equation.

Many abuse victims later confront their abusers face-to-face. In these intense situations, the brains of abuse survivors will likely return to the hyper-aroused states they experienced during their original trauma. This is a necessary step. Intensely raw energies of fight and flight will be awakened simultaneously. Persons about to confront their abusers may fear that they will go insane or even kill someone when these long-buried fight/flight energies flood their minds and bodies. Those who can stay mindful through these intense states, however, create the opportunity to choose responses other than freezing. Adults have more agency than children. They can choose to fight in the face of a former abuser. This does not necessarily mean a fistfight. Often people can fight verbally with words of truth. Adults can also choose flight. Fleeing can simply entail avoiding future contact with abusers. Those who tolerate this extreme discomfort and choose responses other than freezing, renegotiate their survival responses.

Once people chose a new option, such as some manner of fighting or fleeing, their brains will send important signals to their bodies. One signal will be to discharge stored-up freeze energies. This, again, is instinctive. Since the survival brain has now re-negotiated, the energies related to freeze are no longer necessary. The freeze discharge may be very intense. Again, the body may shake uncontrollably for short periods of time. It can feel like an epic panic attack, but the freeze discharge is therapeutic and essential. Persons whose insomnia, stomach disorders, depression, backaches, etc. were related to stored-up freeze energy quickly feel better. The survival brain, in turn, will be free to create new wiring for fight and/or flight response in future situations. New mental maps can be created for recovery and resilience. Protector Parts can also begin to step back. Emotions of anger, fear, hurt and even joy may now be experienced. To be sure, each step in these processes can take time and effort. But Levine's model for PTSD recovery offers much hope and direction to suffering persons.

I have personally seen trauma survivors renegotiating their survival responses. These moments are not easy to forget. As these persons' brains became flooded with raw energy of fight and flight, their eyes took on wild, terrified and hyper-aggressive looks. One young woman tolerated this discomfort long enough to renegotiate a new fight option. A survivor of childhood sexual traumas, she was being sexually harassed by a male authority figure in adulthood. Initially she followed her conditioning and froze in the face of his vulgarities. However, she decided courageously to file complaints against this harasser. Shortly after making her decision to fight, she experienced an intense freeze discharge. Her long-term anxiety/depression symptoms soon improved. A few weeks later I saw a joyful expression on her face for the first time. She had renegotiated.

Persons who suffer from PTSD can have very courageous and chivalrous spirits. For example, I know a man who had developed childhood PTSD after being repeatedly abused by his father. He still loved his father and tried hard to forgive him. His PTSD, however, greatly reduced his quality of life. Whenever this man's raw fight and flight energies would start to resurface, his freeze Protector Parts would take over. His greatest fear was that his buried anger would overtake him and he'd kill his father. This man stayed stuck in freeze for years for the chivalrous reason of not wanting to harm his father. However, once he realised that trauma recovery would allow him to better serve God, he moved toward renegotiating. Principles of chivalry guided his choices in both cases.

Trauma recovery and renegotiation processes are inherently risky. They are best guided by competent trauma recovery counsellors and God. The overall recovery processes involve much more than rewiring survival brains for fighting or fleeing. Each step toward trauma recovery can be exhausting emotionally, mentally and physically. Survivors need stable connections and encouragement for this. One step at a time, survivors also need to trust that they possess enough self-control to not shamefully flee or violently attack. Mentors can offer interactive self-control. In addition, professional support may be needed to help survivors create new meanings from their traumatic experiences.

In many respects, the United States today is a trauma-conducive society. Robert Scaer raised such sociological implications of Levine's theory in his book, *The Trauma Spectrum*. Scaer linked traumas to a wide spectrum of common social circumstances, including childhood attachment issues, chronic poverty, crime victimisation, physical ailments and health insurance binds. In these circumstances people cannot fight or flee their stressors. They may also perceive threats to their ego identity and/or physical life. Scaer argues that PTSD can also result from accumulations of little traumas. Many abuse victims are whittled away at each day by abusers. When such people cannot fight or flee, and believe one more whittle will precipitate ego death, they are susceptible to PTSD.

Scaer asserts that better societal recognition and treatment of hidden trauma is needed in US society. Freeze energies are designed to slow down bodies and minds. To untrained eyes, Post Traumatic Stress Disorder may masquerade as laziness. Yet persons with PTSD need compassion, empathy and recovery options more than they need to be judged or shamed as lazy. Meanwhile problems on structural levels of society, such as those related to the declining middle class and health care, may need to be addressed on these levels to prevent many more citizens falling into a trauma-conducive lifestyle.

Spiritual journeys gift persons with resources that reduce their susceptibility to PTSD. Spiritual identities are much less vulnerable to trauma than are ego identity. I realised this first hand through one of my own challenging experiences. I worked as a Case Manager for persons with developmental disabilities and/or mental illnesses. At the time, my ego derived a strong sense of identity from my role as a protector. I was so driven to ensure that my clients were safe and respected that I dropped by group residences on evenings and weekends. With my ego overly attached to this identity, however, I found it very hard to detach from my job. I did not necessarily know who I was outside of these roles.

Despite my best efforts, a client of mine died from being placed in a very questionable floor restraint that I had formally objected to. Many parts of my personality were impacted. My ego's identity, however, seemed to split into pieces. My ego had defined myself as a protector and, in my mind, I had failed to protect. My vengeful Protector Parts took the wheel for a while. I did not move toward healing until I invited God, and my own spirit, into the equations. Through God my spiritual identity is able to transcend earthly roles and outcomes. Today when my more spirit-led self assumes a protective role, I identify myself as an instrument of a Higher Power. I am better able to let go of outcomes. Incidents of abuse to vulnerable persons still enrage my soul. But my spirit's identity is not vulnerable to fragmentation, in the face of inability to protect, like my ego once was.

Aware that the spirit cannot be destroyed, journeyers experience fewer traumatic reactions. Again, the gift of individualised divine consciousness allows journeyers to see their spiritual identities as real, valid and worthwhile regardless of outcomes. Journeyers who conquer their fear of physical death, to some degree, can also circumvent traumas. In addition, the spiritual armour of God also protects journeyers from being traumatised. Those who put on the belt of truth, the breastplate of righteousness, the sandals of peace, the shield of faith and the helmet of salvation (Ephesians 6:10-18) can protect their true selves from a host of threats. Wielding the sword of the Spirit, God's word, journeyers can also take the offensive against bullies who may otherwise wish to negate fight or flight options.

Even trauma recovery on the spiritual journey falls shy of one-hundred percent. Some residual pains and angst may persist long after freeze energies have been discharged. Unhealed wounds may transform into guides. Yet if journeyers have renegotiated their survival-brain responses, discharged freeze energies, developed new mental maps for future coping, recovered Exiled personality parts, transformed Protectors and found meaning and opportunity amid their crises, they have transcended their traumas. Any future flashbacks will trigger less intense emotions and arousal states. Inner peace will no longer be disrupted by bad memories. The recovery process, however, cannot be forced to fit any conventional timeline. People tend to recover when God is ready for them to.

As mentioned, Protector and Exiled Parts wish to be heard and validated by someone. Almost anyone can learn to validate someone else's wounds and, for that matter, resiliencies. On a larger level, numerous benefits could result from a society that better validates wounds and resilience. Validations of wounds facilitate their healing. Greater validation of resilience increases people's ability to survive, thrive and solve problems. Validation of the human heart, in turn, could increase the likelihood that persons choose noble journeys over paths of idolatry. The converse, however, can also be true. If resilience and recovery potential is invalidated or dismissed, it may not be utilised. Numerous people who suffer may be discouraged from choosing spiritual paths. They may simply take meds.

The last two chapters described processes associated with transcending trauma and transforming shadows. It is worth emphasising, though, that processes of healing, recovery, renegotiation and transformation run counter to dominant cultural values. These processes are neither efficient nor immediately gratifying. They do not necessarily generate social status, or lead to financial gain. Since recovery processes lead toward authenticity and holism, they may be seen as threatening to narcissistic and dogmatic factions. Spiritual journeys themselves challenge prevalent views of PTSD and mental illness as not being recoverable; as requiring medication for life.

Those whose spirits travel against these cultural currents, however, will gain in all levels of being. Their overall personalities and use of perspectives will become more whole. Journeyers will notice greater love, self-confidence, courage, energy, compassion, intelligence, freedom from the past, etc. When people no longer experience intense fears, rages, or anxieties, self-control rapidly increases. Spiritual journeyers gain powerful blends of acquired and inherent resiliencies. A sense of calling facilitates better connection with God, Christ and the Holy Spirit. They serve God with more meaning, joy, hope and purpose.

On the noble journey, shadow work and trauma recovery also lead to spiritual chivalry. Trauma and sin can drive persons to God, the ultimate source of spiritual chivalry. Trauma recovery also prompts parts and shadow work. Personality parts are given new opportunities to heal and transform in ways that facilitate spiritual chivalry. Self-compassion is conducive to spiritual chivalry. It facilitates chivalrous transformations of Protector Parts and Exiles. Spirits gain more mastery of the overall personality. They can lead the whole self toward more chivalrous actions in the world in the service of God. Journeyers also gain more empathy and compassion for persons who are suffering. They can offer and receive more chivalrous support and resources to others in need. Many noble soul relationships are borne of trauma recovery.

(15)

An Awakening of Spiritual Chivalry

One of the most awe-inspiring accounts of Joseph Campbell's "road of trials" stage of a noble journey, that I am aware of, comes from the failed Antarctic expedition of Sir Ernest Shackleton. Ernest Shackleton hoped to be the first explorer to cross the continent of Antarctica. Several had tried before him. In 1914 Shackleton set sail from England with two ships and 56 men. Each ship went to a different side of the continent. In January of 1915, however, Shackleton's ship *Endurance* became trapped in ice that had engulfed it. For months it slowly drifted while Shackleton and crew camped on surrounding ice plateaus. In October of 1915, the *Endurance* began to take in water, sinking the next month.

For the next several months, Shackleton and crew hoped the ice they resided on would drift 250 miles to Paulet Island. The ice raft, however, eventually broke in two. Shackleton and his 27 crewmembers boarded their lifeboats. After sailing five days they landed on Elephant Island, nearly 350 miles from where the *Endurance* sank. The crew had not stood on solid ground for a year and a half. Unfortunately, Elephant Island was far removed from shipping routes. Their odds of rescue were slim to none. Shackleton decided to attempt what is still seen today as an almost impossible navigational feat. Taking five men with him in a modified lifeboat, Shackleton sailed 720 nautical miles toward a whaling station on South Georgia.

Unfortunately, Shackleton's lifeboat landed on the wrong side of South Georgia. Shackleton took two men with him on another impossible trek. The three of them spent the next day and a half crossing mountainous terrain so treacherous that indigenous persons considered it a "no man's land". They did not stop for fear of freezing to death. Upon reaching the whaling station, Shackleton persevered through several failed attempts to rescue his crew from Elephant Island. Eventually, Shackleton found a Chilean tugboat to pick up his stranded men. Everyone in Shackleton's party survived the ordeal. They arrived home in England in time to volunteer to join their countrymen in the trenches of WWI.

I see Shackleton's journey as not just an amazing resilience and survival story, but one of notably spiritual chivalry as well. Initially Ernest Shackleton was driven by egoistic concerns to explore Antarctica. He sought the fame and glory of being the first to cross the continent. One the *Endurance* sank, however, Shackleton's priorities shifted. He became single-minded in his intention to bring his entire crew home alive—a noble endeavour. Shackleton maintained that purpose through countless trails and disappointments. Later he summed up these experiences: 'We had pierced the veneer of outside things. We had suffered, starved and triumphed, grovelled down yet grasped at glory, grown bigger in the bigness of the whole. We had seen God in His splendour, heard the text that nature renders. We had reached the naked soul of man.'

Leadership was clearly one of Sir Ernest Shackleton's gifts of spirit. His leadership methods are still widely studied today. Shackleton modelled and inspired optimism. He never let his crew know when his own confidence waned. Shackleton also assigned daily duties to each of his men, giving them structure while uniting them with a sense of purpose. To further build unity, he insisted that his men socialise with each other after dinner. Shackleton modelled principled decisions. He and his carpenter carried animosity for each other. For the good of everyone's survival, both men chivalrously put their feelings aside to join forces and sail to South Georgia.

Human history offers an encyclopaedia of human actions that have been egregious, or have exemplified spiritual chivalry. Some persons have been honoured or sainted for their triumphs of spirit. The spiritual valour of many others remains unsung. Noble journeys begin when false selves fail, as John Eldredge proposes. The loss of one's persona prompts human hearts to make very important choices. Persons can choose to reinvent their false selves and continue on paths of self-centredness and idolatry. Or they can instead choose to step bravely into unknowns, awakening to spiritual chivalry. Roads of trails can certainly prompt these choices. Our youth today, surrounded by information technology, may see less need for spiritual chivalry than did St Ignatius of Loyola in his hospital bed; or Shackleton and crew when stranded on an Antarctic ice block. Should youth of today choose to seek their calls, however, their own noble journeys would lead them to challenging contexts that prompt their own fateful heart choices.

At this very moment in history, thousands of people worldwide are putting their unique chivalries of spirit into action. Some are chivalrously offering services, hope, advocacy and compassion to people in need. Others are helping to heal the wounded through medicine, counselling and faith. Others yet are chivalrously risking their lives to protect the innocent, and their communities, from ominous threats. Parents worldwide are sacrificing in large and small ways for their children. When persons set aside cynicism, and open their eyes to spiritual chivalry, they begin to see examples of it all around. A path of spiritual chivalry may begin with one's first choice to serve a higher cause. Like a muscle, however, the will to serve with spiritual chivalry gets stronger through use.

Sparks of spiritual chivalry lit in one person can ignite similar sparks in others. Shackleton and his crew discovered this. St Ignatius of Loyola, ignited by the examples of Christ, inspired spiritual chivalry in those he encountered. Athletic teams and military squads frequently experience a proliferation of spiritual chivalry. Classic American films paid frequent tribute to this phenomenon. Collective spiritual chivalry also emerges in healthy workplaces, churches, social movements, community responses to crises, family events, etc. A critical number of group members, however, need adequate foundations of resilience in place for spiritual chivalry to translate into purposeful actions.

The converse, however, is also true. At this moment many persons worldwide are thinking and behaving in ways antithetical to spiritual chivalry. Ignobility can beget ignobility. In chapter one I raised two "how" questions. In one I asked,

'How can people best progress on their spiritual paths in a culture that often normalises narcissism, mediocrity and mean-spiritedness?' A lot of suggestions have been offered throughout this book. Keeping one's compass set toward God, and one's calling, helps journeyers persevere on more spiritually chivalrous paths. It is important to choose friendships with others who are chivalrous in spirit. The armour of God is available for journeyers called upon to enter snake pits. Individualised divine consciousness allows journeyers to be aware of their own spiritual chivalry even if others dismiss or invalidate it. Journeyers can treat wounds and Protector Parts with compassion, even if this is not a cultural norm. Protector Parts transform in ways contributing to chivalry. When the spirit takes the helm, it ennobles the overall personality through connections with God's divine love and chivalry. And it helps to know that, unlike ego chivalry, the human spirit can never be destroyed.

Putting such knowledge into action cannot help but to advance the causes of spiritual chivalry. In chapter one I also asked, 'How do people maintain enough ego to navigate and manage very complicated lives, yet still develop in their spirits and souls?' Again, the ego is an important navigator and Protector Part. It allows persons who have not awakened spiritually to function. Journeyers need to respect their egos. They can do so without making idols out of them or demonising them. By dialoguing with one's ego from a place of respect, compassion and curiosity, journeyers help egos transition to advisory roles more conducive to chivalry for the overall personality. Transformed egos still lend resiliencies, strengths, coping, etc. to spirit-led selves.

Holism has been a consistent theme of this book. Walks with God are integrative. Journeyers' resilience, for example, becomes more whole. Learned and/or inborn resilience qualities eventually blend with inherently resilient qualities of awakened spirits and souls. Spirits and souls, through a shared sense of calling, align in nobler ways. Through and/both thinking, a journeyer's use of conventional perspectives and worldviews become more holistic. Journeyers continue to draw truths and methods from conventional perspectives, while transcending unnecessary divisions. Independent and interactive self-control systems integrate as well. In their best moments, journeyers feel chivalrously independent and inter-dependent at the same time.

Paradoxical qualities of journeyers also integrate. As mentioned, Al Siebert emphasised how resilient people can be tough and soft, masculine and feminine, vulnerable and indomitable at the same time. Journeyers can begin to ask, 'When it is chivalrous to be kind?' and, 'When is it chivalrous to be tough?' Answers to these questions help integrate one's paradoxical qualities. Similarly, when journeyers' spirits and souls align, they feel paradoxically calm and uplifted at the same time. Calmness comes from peaceful depths of transformation within the soul. Converted spirits lift people up. Strong connections with the Holy Spirit facilitate these processes. Noble journeys integrate countless other opposites as well. Overall journeys blend periods of activity with non-activity. They incorporate moments of relative control as well as surrender. Journeyers think rationally and non-rationally. They are scientific and religious. In following their spiritual compasses toward God, journeyers can be conformists and non-conformists. Able to connect with people from many walks of life, journeyers can also walk alone.

Through individualised divine consciousness, spirit-led journeyers form their own unique perspectives. These, too, are holistic. Each journeyer becomes better able to see the influence of God and His glory in distinctive ways. Because God's glory exists in infinite manifestations, no one's perspective can comprehend all of His shades, colours and nuances. The world needs a lot of perspectives from a lot of spiritual journeyers to bring more dimensions of divine glory to light. With that said, journeyers increasingly expand their abilities to see, respect and validate a wide range of Godly qualities in others. As they increasingly identify with other chivalrous journeyers across social lines, new opportunities for respect and validation arise. As chivalrous qualities become more respected and validated in others, they can become more powerful and consequential. If more people across the globe adopted and/both perspectives, the world would be in better position to solve its formidable problems.

Journeyers' and/both perspectives are individualistic and collectivistic at the same time. Journeyers respect chivalrous individuals walking their own distinct paths. They also respect complex, inter-connected relationships of groups, social systems and structures. En route to spiritual self-mastery (individualism), journeyers choose to serve causes higher than themselves (collectivism). Similarly, journeyers' perspectives are objective and subjective. An objective component stems from a culturally universal premise; that is, all lives are geared toward spiritual journeys. Objectivity can also consider similarities and differences in journeys as related to gender, culture, socio-economic status, sexual orientation, race/ethnicity, birth order, occupation, religious denomination, rural and urban environments, historical contexts, etc. On the other hand, a subjective component creates understandings of the more distinct challenges of particular journeyers. Subjective views can see chivalric uniqueness in each person's path toward God.

Noble journeyers are quick to make lemonade out of lemons, failures and transgressions. Many recovering addicts and alcoholics, for example, journey to become chemical-dependency sponsors and counsellors. In doing so they put their previous experiences with addictive behaviours, withdrawal, despair, etc. to good use. Chapter thirteen discussed how sinful and/or negative personality parts can be transformed. Generally speaking, journeyers' perspectives find constructive uses for almost any strength or skill once used for dysfunctional purposes. The mental resources that once helped addicts score drugs, for example, may later be applied toward solving growth and recovery problems. Many addicts also possess strong skills for reading peoples' vulnerabilities. A practising addict may use these skills for exploitative and manipulative purposes. A journeying addict turned sponsor, on the other hand, may apply the same skills toward discerning how to best guide and empower people in need.

Journeyers' perspectives also transcend cultural proclivities for fearing, hating and/or disrespecting people who are struggling or simply different. As mentioned, I believe the largest difference between people is not based on race, gender, socio-economic status, or the like. It is instead based on whether or not they choose to journey. A lot of non-journeying Americans express contempt for impoverished and disadvantaged citizens. Low-income and homeless Americans are sometimes uniformly labelled as lazy. Journeyers can indeed discern sins of laziness when they are existent, but they can also understand trauma. PTSD can appear as laziness to untrained eyes. Many traumatised persons already have strikes against them. In addition to being shut down by the freeze response, they may lack the social networks, educational credentials and/or coping resources to rise above their situation. Noble journeyers are able to note the many internal and external variables that can influence earthly outcomes. Journeyers also see that small acts of respect, compassion and mercy motivate growth much better than mistreatment and/or contempt.

I still think about random acts of kindness I experienced when I was homeless over 25 years ago. To share one story, I moved to Seattle in the early 1990s when it was popular destination. Jobs quickly became scarce. Unable to keep my apartment, I decided to hitchhike down coastal highways to Portland, Eugene and finally California. In San Francisco, I found myself lost in a high-crime neighbourhood in the middle of the night. While searching for a place to sleep, I felt eyes on the back of my neck from packs of young males roaming the night. The alleys were locked up. Options for a safe sleep seemed scarce. Finally, I stumbled onto an apartment complex. The door to the laundry room was unlocked. Inside I spread out my sleeping bag on the folding table and lay down. I planned to be up and out of there before sunrise.

Having run on adrenaline for several days, though, I went out cold. I woke up to a dark-haired, middle-aged man prodding my foot with a long stick. This apartment manager told me nervously that I must leave. Feeling embarrassed and guilty, I apologised. I told him I would be gone in five minutes. He left the room. Within perhaps two minutes, however, this man returned with a cup of coffee and a chocolate birthday cake. He handed them to me. He kept repeating, 'Take it, take it, take it, you need it more than me.' The birthday cake had a boy's name on it. I didn't want to deprive a child of his/her birthday cake, but the man insisted. I was deeply touched and inspired by his kindness. Although I was agnostic at the time, I sensed a chivalrous Godly presence in this man and his actions. While homeless, I also encountered a lot of violence, contempt and incivility from hyper-conventional persons. It never led to positive change. Chivalric kindness, however, stopped me in my tracks. It ignited a spark inside of me to live a better life. The memory of this man's kind actions inspires me to this day.

Today my journey perspective often advises me to offer similar support to others. I try to do so without letting my ego attach to particular outcomes. My ego used to become very disappointed when, say, alcoholics I tried to help still continued to drink and/or engage in unhealthy behaviours (Protector Parts). One opportunity for me amid these situations, though, was to learn to defer the ultimate outcomes to God. When I offer support from this higher perspective today, I connect more with God's will more than I do my ego's. This allows my ego to remain unattached. My spirit stays at the helm. My "and/both" perspective also recognises the need for tough love at times.

Some agnostics have implied that they think deferring outcomes to God means one turns his/her back on social injustices. God does allow social evils to exist for numerous reasons, many of them mysterious to me. Acknowledging this is not the same thing as condoning human evil. On His timelines, God calls upon journeyers to chivalrously address social evils and injustices. Journeys can become gifted in the very places they were once wounded. For example, many journeys include early experiences of childhood abuses. Their journeys transform these wounds into life lessons. These journeyers may later be called upon to use their strengths, experiences and spiritual gifts to address child abuse as counsellors, attorneys, protective services workers and police officers.

Although journeyers' perspectives can take them to great spiritual heights, they also respect limits and limitations. American culture promotes many "no limits" marketing slogans. Many Americans assert, 'You can do anything you set your mind to doing.'

While not totally disagreeing I would add, 'But you cannot do everything you set your mind to do.' Only so many skills can be mastered in one lifetime. Also, as mentioned, limits placed on spiritual transcendence can make soul relationships possible and vice versa. Almost everyone I know is trying to transcend something in his/her life, albeit addiction, poverty, childhood deprivation, depression, over-eating, sin, etc. If journeyers fully transcended all of their barriers tomorrow, they may not develop the deep connections—borne of their arduous efforts to transcend—that ennoble their souls. I am not, however, advocating for giving up on efforts to transcend. Our spirits are designed for this.

Human struggles for chivalric freedoms have existed in every era. So have callings to sacrifice for these and other higher causes. Perhaps only the particularities of human sacrifice and struggle change from generation to generation. Sometimes I reflect upon the journeys of the WWII generation. I started working, and attended college, when members of this generation still served as professors, bosses, co-workers, etc. Their collective chivalrous accomplishments included enduring the Great Depression, helping liberate the world from tyranny and building a middle-class society. Most everyone followed cultural norms of chivalry. Yet for so many, chivalry was very spiritual. As a generation they triumphed with humility and quiet honour. To be sure, I have met many veterans of other wars, and many journeyers who are not veterans, who possess similar qualities. The chivalry of the WWII generation, however, seemed to be woven into the fabric of the overall culture. It embodied many truths. People are often called upon to sacrifice for the greater good. Freedom and transcendence can come at great costs.

These truths persist. Today's spiritual journeyers face different sets of challenges. Among these are climate changes, a diminishing middle class, fierce global economic competition, terrorism, rising world populations, etc. These challenges may necessitate different skill sets. Journeyers today may be asked for more autonomy, flexibility, entrepreneurship and imagination than were many of their predecessors. Nonetheless, any journeyer in any culture or era can make heart choices to move in Godly directions of spiritual chivalry. The unique and universal triumphs of every journeyer, or generation of journeyers, can inspire chivalrous honour, resilience, courage, sacrifice, etc. in countless others. Like the WWII generation, today's journeyers can develop inter-connections that advance collective interests. Today's journeyers can live freely with spiritual masteries and shared soulful missions at the same time. Their overall cultures can move toward slightly different manifestations of chivalry; ones that suit the changing times.

Deepak Chopra offers the saying, 'When you follow your dharma the universe responds.' Any heartfelt choice taken in the direction of a calling will somehow be responded to by God (in His many names). God may respond by sending new mentors. Journeyers may experience "chance encounters" with others that open new doors of opportunities. Right now, anyone can find a first or next step to take. Over time momentum for the spiritual journey is generated by a succession of such steps. But for whatever individual journeyers do or do not ultimately accomplish, their inherently chivalrous spirit will be ennobled by God. A little bit of His noble glory will become theirs. This, I believe, is an eternal essence of Heaven. Meanwhile, millions of new journeyers will be called upon to accomplish what previous generations were not meant to. Their hearts can choose chivalry today.

References

Alexander, Eben. (2012). *Proof of Heaven: A Neurosurgeon's Journey into the Afterlife.* New York, N.Y.: Simon and Schuster.

Bakhtiar, Laleh. (1994). *Moral Healer's Handbook: The Psychology of Spiritual Chivalry.* Volume II of God's Will Be Done. Chicago, Il: The Institute of Traditional Psychoethics and Guidance.

Baumeister, Roy F. (1999). *Evil: Inside Human Violence and Cruelty.* New York, N.Y.: Henry Holt & Company LLC.

Baumeister, Roy F., and Tierney, John. (1994). *Willpower: Rediscovering the Greatest Human Strength.* New York, N.Y.: Penguin Press HC.

Campbell, Joseph. (1968). *The Hero with a Thousand Faces* (2nd Ed.). Princeton, N.J.: Princeton University Press.

Chopra, Deepak. (2004). *The Book of Secrets: Unlocking the Hidden Dimensions of Your Life.* New York, N.Y.: Harmony Books.

Dahm, K., Meyer, E.C., Neff, K., Kimbrel, N.A., Gulliver, S.B., & Morissette, S.B. (2015). "Mindfulness, Self-compassion, Posttraumatic Stress Disorder Symptoms, and Functional Disability in US Iraq and Afghanistan War Veterans." *Journal of Traumatic Stress,* 28, 460-464.

Desai, Panache. (2014). *Discovering Your Soul Signature: A 33-Day Path to Purpose, Passion, and Joy.* New York, N.Y.: Random House LLC.

Eldredge, John. (2006). *Waking the Dead: The Glory of a Heart Fully Alive.* Nashville, TN: Thomas Nelson.

Eldredge, John. (2010). *Wild at Heart Revised and Updated: Discovering the Secret of Man's Soul.* Nashville, TN: Thomas Nelson.

Frankl, Viktor. (1997). *Man's Search for Meaning* (Standard Ed.). New York, N.Y.: Washington Square Press.

Gonzales, Laurence. (2003). *Deep Survival: Who Lives, Who Dies, and Why.* New York: W.W Norton.

Gottfredson, Michael, and Hirschi, Travis. (1990). *A General Theory of Crime.* Stanford, CA: Stanford University Press.

Greene, Todd W. (2012). "A Paradox of Street Survival: Street Masteries Influencing Runaways' Motivations to Maintain Street Life." *Theory in Action 5(3): 31-57.*

Hoffer, Eric. (1951). *The True Believer.* New York, N.Y.: Harper & Row Publishers.

Hedges, Chris. (2010). *Empire of Illusion: The End of Literacy and the Triumph of Spectacle.* New York, N.Y.: Perseus Books Group.

Jung, Carl G. (2006). *The Undiscovered Self* (Reissue Ed.). New York, N.Y.: The Penguin Group.

Laing, R.D. (1965). *The Divided Self: An Existential Study in Sanity and Madness.* New York, N.Y.: The Penguin Group.

Levine, Peter. (1997). *Waking the Tiger: Healing Trauma.* Berkeley, CA: North Atlantic Books.

Mandela, Nelson. (1994). *Long Walk to Freedom: The Autobiography of Nelson Mandela.* Boston, MA: Little, Brown, & Company.

McNab, Chris. (2004). *How to Survive Anything, Anywhere: A Handbook of Survival Skills for Every Scenario and Environment.* Camden, ME: International Marine/Rugged Mountain Press.

Mooney, Edward F. (1991). *Knights of Faith and Resignation: Reading Kierkegaard's Fear and Trembling.* Albany, N.Y.: SUNY Press.

Moore, Robert L. (2003). *Facing the Dragon: Confronting Personal and Spiritual Grandiosity.* Asheville, N.C.: Chiron Publications.

Moore, Robert, and Gillette, Douglas. (1991). *King, Warrior, Magician, Lover: Rediscovering the Archetypes of the Mature Masculine.* San Francisco, CA: HarperCollins.

Morrell, Margot, and Caperrell, Stephanie. (2002). *Shackleton's Way: Leadership Lessons from the Great Antarctic Explorer.* London: Penguin Books.

Munroe, Myles. (2005). *The Glory of Living: Keys to Releasing Your Personal Glory.* Shippensburg, PA: Destiny Image Publishers Inc.

Ogden, Pat, Pain, Clare, and Minton, Kekuni. (2006). *Trauma and the Body: A Sensorimotor Approach to Psychotherapy.* New York, N.Y.: W. W. Norton & Company.

Peck, M. Scott. (1992). *The Road Less Traveled: A New Psychology of Love, Traditional Values and Spiritual Growth.* New York N. Y.: Simon & Schuster.

Reivich, Karen, and Shatte, Andrew. (2003). *The Resilience Factor: 7 Keys to Finding Your Inner Strength and Overcoming Life's Hurdles.* New York, N.Y.: Harmony Books.

Rhodes, Susan. (2010). *Archetypes of the Enneagram: Exploring the Life Themes of the 27 Enneagram Subtypes from the Perspective of the Soul.* Seattle, W.A.: Geranium Press.

Rohr, Richard. (2103). *Immortal Diamond: The Search For Our True Self.* San Francisco, CA: Jossey-Bass.

Scaer, Robert. (2005). *The Trauma Spectrum: Hidden Wounds and Human Resiliency.* New York: W. W. Norton & Company.

Schore, Allan N. (1994). *Affect Regulation and the Origin of the Self: The Neurobiology of Emotional Development.* Hillsdale, N.J.: Lawrence Erlbaum Associates Inc.

Schwartz, Richard C., and Falconer, Robert R. (2017). *Many Minds, One Self: Evidence for a Radical Shift in Paradigm.* Oak Park, Il: Trailheads Publications.

Schweitzer, Albert. (1969). *Reverence for Life* (Later print Ed.). New York, N.Y.: Harper & Row.

Scott, Robert Lee. (1983). *God is My Co-Pilot.* New York, N.Y.: Ballantine Books.

Siebert, Al. (1996). *Survivor Personality: Why Some People Are Stronger, Smarter, and More Skillful at Handling Life's Difficulties...and How You Can Be, Too.* New York, N.Y.: The Berkley Publishing Group.

Southwick, Steven M., and Charney, Dennis S. (2012). *Resilience: The Science of Mastering Life's Greatest Challenges.* New York, N.Y.: Cambridge University Press.

Triandis, Harry C. (1995). *Individualism and Collectivism* (New Directions in Social Psychology). Boulder, CO: Westview Press.

Twenge, Jean M. (2017). *iGen: Why Today's Super-Connected Kids Are Growing Up Less Rebellious, More Tolerant, Less Happy—and Completely Unprepared for Adulthood—and What That Means for the Rest of Us.* New York, N.Y.: Atria Books (2nd Print edition).

Twenge, Jean M., and Campbell, W. Keith. (2010). *The Narcissism Epidemic: Living in the Age of Entitlement.* New York, N.Y.: Atria.

Vaknin, Sam. (2015). *Malignant Self-Love: Narcissism Revisited* (Revised Ed.). Czech Republic: Narcissus Publications.

Wagner, Tony. (2010). *The Global Achievement Gap: Why Even Our Best Schools Don't Teach the New Survival Skills Our Children Need—and What We Can Do About It.* New York, N.Y.: Basic Books.

Wicks, Robert J. (2003). *Riding the Dragon: 10 Lessons for Inner Strength in Challenging Times.* Notre Dame, IN: Sorin Books.

Woodruff, Paul. (2014). *Reverence: Renewing a Forgotten Virtue* (2nd Ed.). Oxford: Oxford University Press.

Woodward, John B. (2000). *Man as Spirit, Soul, and Body: A Study of Biblical Psychology* (Revised Ed.). Grace Fellowship International.